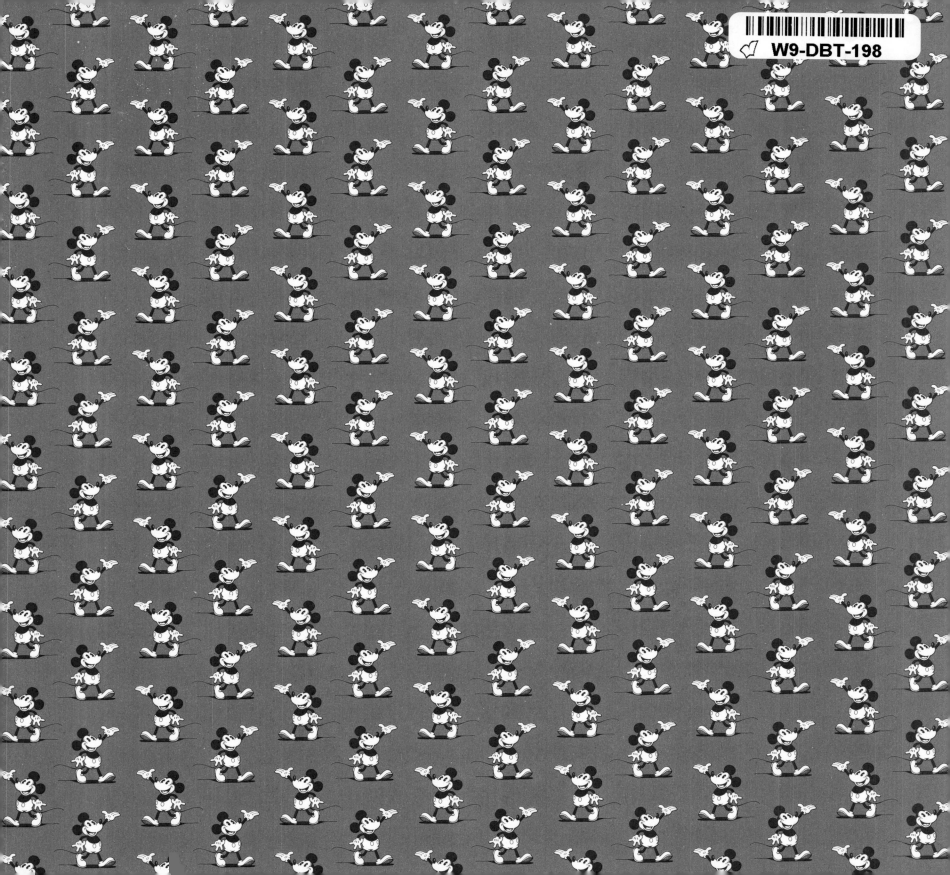

W9-DBT-198

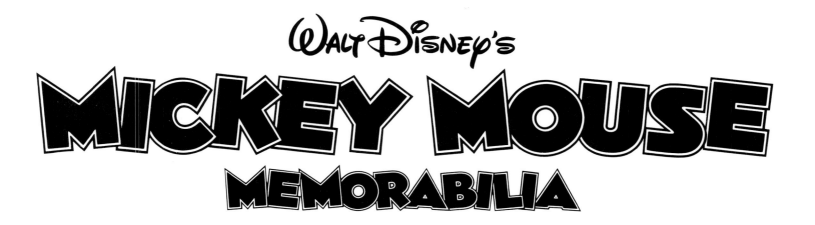

Walt Disney's MICKEY MOUSE MEMORABILIA

THE VINTAGE YEARS 1928-1938

INTRODUCTION: BEVIS HILLIER
PRINCIPAL CONSULTANT: BERNARD C. SHINE

HARRY N. ABRAMS, INC., PUBLISHERS, NEW YORK

Library of Congress Cataloging-in-Publication Data

Walt Disney's Mickey Mouse memorabilia.

   Bibliography: p.
   Includes index.
   1. Mickey Mouse (Cartoon character)—Collectibles. 2.
Walt Disney Productions—Collectibles. 3. Shine,
Bernard—Art collections. 4. Birnkrant, Mel—Art
collections. 5. Novelties—Private collections—United
States. I. Hillier, Bevis, 1940–
NK808.W34 1986   741.5'09794'93   86-3391
ISBN 0-8109-1439-5

Copyright © 1986 The Walt Disney Company
Published in 1986 by Harry N. Abrams, Incorporated,
New York
All rights reserved. No part of the contents of this book
may be reproduced without the written permission of the
publishers

Times Mirror Books

Produced by the Justin Knowles Publishing Group
9 Colleton Crescent, Exeter, Devon EX2 4BY, U.K.

Designed by Tim Harvey

Typesetting by P&M Typesetting Ltd, Exeter, Devon, U.K.

Printed and bound in Hong Kong

Jacket illustrations: *front:* Mickey and Minnie dolls made
by Charlotte Clark during the 1930s from the Ward
Kimball Collection. *Back* Celluloid figures and wind-up
toys made between 1931 and 1937 from the Mel
Birnkrant Collection. *Spine* The illustration of Mickey that
appeared inside the box containing Ingersoll's de luxe
Mickey Mouse watch.

CONTENTS

ACKNOWLEDGEMENTS

This book would never have existed in this form had it not been for the cooperation and support of many people.

The principal consultant, Bernard C. Shine, who generously made available his manuscript "Mickey Memories from the Vintage Years," not only allowed us access to his fine collection but also showed endless patience in dealing with innumerable queries. Mel Birnkrant's profound knowledge, combined with his collection of items of the finest quality, is one of the key aspects of the book. Other major collectors who have permitted us to feature items from their collections include Robert Lesser, Stefan Raia Sztybel, Lynn Trickett and the Walt Disney Archives.

Ward Kimball, a unique figure in Disney history, has provided an additional dimension to many aspects of the book. As well as allowing us to photograph items from his collection, Ward has communicated in his highly individual Preface something of the magic of this vintage period. Bevis Hillier has contributed an innovatory and stimulating introduction.

Led by the expert knowledge of Archivist David R. Smith, the Archives of the Walt Disney Company have provided invaluable information, especially for the section on publications. In addition to Dave Smith's encouragement, there has been much consistent support from the Walt Disney Company as a whole: Keith Bales, Armand Bigle, Bo Boyd, Greg Crosby, Wendall Mohler and Wayne Morris.

This has not been an easy book to produce, and much credit must go to all those who have been involved. Richard Holliss and Brian Sibley have contributed their specialist knowledge; Susan Brown Nicholson was an enthusiastic consultant editor; and Graham Strong took the excellent photographs. Special thanks are due to the designer, Tim Harvey.

The commitment shown toward this work by all the publishers is greatly appreciated, but in particular the participation of Paul Gottlieb and Darlene Geis of Harry N. Abrams, Inc., will always be recognized.

Our intention in producing this book has been to communicate the visual quality of the images of Mickey produced during the vintage years and to bring their excellence as objects in their own right before a wider audience. Although most of the items illustrated on the pages that follow are extremely rare, do not be deterred from collecting examples of Mickey merchandise from this classic era.

Since its conception some years ago, this book has become something of a personal obsession with me, and to all of you who have contributed to its publication — thank you.

Justin Knowles

NOTE:
This is letterhead
we used in 1934!
← when I
started working
at Disneys
W.K.

Justin Knowles
42 Barnsbury St.

London, England

March, 1986
Ward Kimball

Dear Justin:

Without benefit of Halucinogenic chemicals or hypnotic memory aids and solely prompted by my electronic Ouija board, I invite you to indulge in a little time warpage as I try to picture for you some of my thoughts and experiences as a young art student aspiring to be a film animator at the Walt Disney studio during the Great Depression of the 1930's. I hope this nostalgic letter stationery helps frame the scene for you.

Mickey Mouse was only six years old when I struggled to make my first inbetween drawing of him for a short film, "Orphans Benefit". I was an apprentice under an assistant animator who showed me some of the early tricks in drawing Mickey. He explained that Mickey was roughly 3½ heads tall, using equal size circles to construct his head and lower torso. I noted early that no matter which way Mickey turned his head, his two ball-shaped ears floated back and forth on top of his noggin like wayward tennis balls. Aha! I surmised that Mickey wasn't a real mouse at all, he was just a symbolistic abstraction we called a mouse! Maybe this was why we early Disney artists were so critical of the Mickey and Minnie merchandise toys not looking like our animated versions. The three dimensional toys all had round FLAT, "realistic" ears which,when turned in perspective, became thin wafers like real mouse ears. However, in spite of the ear contradiction, when in 1935 I first spied the new Mickey and Minnie Lionel handcar in the Disney studio showcase with an employee's discount tag of only 75¢, I just couldn't resist. Later, I blew part of my meager salary on the Mickey Mouse circus train set, discounted to $1.50. I guess I excused my decisions to acquire these questionable Mouse conceptions because of an all consuming interest in my railroad hobby. Was this the fateful moment when I became a bonified Disneyana collector?

During the 1930's when Kay Kamen was handling the Disney Merchandising business, he would occasionally stop by the animation building to distribute some samples of the latest Mickey Mouse toy creations to us animators. "Here's something for your kids", he'd say. Even though I protested that I as yet didn't have any offspring, Kay would reply,"Well, then maybe these will bring you luck" and he would put the toys on my table anyway! Sometimes I would give these Mickey offerings to neighborhood kids, but most of the time, believe it or not, I dumped these future collectors items in the waste basket. (Eat your heart out, Justin!)

It wasn't until the late 1960's when I produced the Disney TV show celebrating Mickey's 40th birthday that the full import of my early tragic trashing of Mickey momentos hit me. While scouting around secondhand stores for Mickey memorabilia to illustrate a musical toy section in the show, I was shocked to find wrist watches already asking $100 and Mickey handcars priced at $150. At least I could take solace in the thought that I had the foresight to save a few Disney items, including some gifts to wife Betty and the kids: the Charlotte Clark Mickey, Minnie, Donald and Goofy dolls.

THIS IS FIRST LETTERHEAD! →

WALT DISNEY STUDIO
MICKEY MOUSE
SOUND CARTOONS
2719 HYPERION
HOLLYWOOD

I guess Mickey's days as a super, hell-bent-for-leather film star are over. Why was he gradually eclipsed by the new personalities of the short tempered Donald Duck, the bumbling Goofy, the dog antics of Pluto? Why was Mickey, after his early action packed adventure rolls, relegated to sissy, do-gooder parts? We animators used to argue about this situation. Perhaps there are these reasons to consider: Mickey's size, for instance. How could he be accepted as true mouse when his relative size proportions in his film appearances with duck size Donald, man size Goofy and dog size Pluto obviously made Mickey appear to be at least THREE FEET TALL? Think about it! After the instant success of cantankerous Donald, Walt Disney began to build his films around strong, believable personalities, like the Seven Dwarfs in Snow White and the many character personalities in the feature films that followed. Along with the new accent on personality development, Walt was demanding more and more realism in the drawing and the animation of the characters, like the caricatured "real" mice in Cinderella. Mickey, with his falsetto voice, phoney ears and his three foot size, became sort of an animation misfit. On film, he faded slowly into the sunset.

But, hold on! In the other world of character merchandising, Mickey Mouse has never lost his magnetic attraction, especially for the very young who early on are mesmerized by that black and white smiling face with the big ears. He may be getting more pudgy faced now, with his early rubber hose arms and legs covered with layers of more modest clothing, but he is still being loved and collected more than ever. Take my humble advice:
DON'T TOSS YOUR MICKEYS IN THE WASTE BASKET AS I FOOLISHLY DID IN THE 1930's!

Cordially,
Yours,
Yours Truly,
Very Truly Yours,

Your Friend,
Sincerely Yours,
Your Ob'd't Servant,
Thank You.

WARD KIMBALL

GRIZZLY FLATS RAILROAD CO.

COMPARATIVE SIZES
GOOFY, MICKEY, DONALD, PLUTO

MICKEY'S "FLOATING" EARS

FRONT   3/4   PROFILE   3/4 REAR   BACK (EARS SAME AS FRONT)

FIRST DESIGN FOR FIRST MICKEY MOUSE
TOY EVER MADE
DRAWN BY GILLETT

INTRODUCTION

Bevis Hillier

Page 10: Disney artist Burton "Bert" Gillett designed what is thought to have been the first Mickey Mouse toy ever manufactured. The wooden toy, made in 1930, was distributed by the George Borgfeldt Corporation.

My introduction to Mickey Mouse took place when I was only a few months old – before I knew who I was, let alone who *he* was. The year was 1940. The British Government feared that the Germans might use poison gas on civilians, so all adults were supplied with gas masks and required by law to carry them wherever they went. Ronald Blythe, author of *Akenfield* (1969), remembers one *grande dame* who carried hers "in a smart leatherette case with 'Mrs. E. Smith, O.B.E.' inscribed on it in fluorescent paint."[1]

Gas masks were dehumanizing and rather frightening to young children. So a special "Mickey Mouse" gas mask was designed for children, to make poison gas drill seem fun, like a party game. One of these was clamped on my face, and in a moment of rubbery inhalation (which the dentist's mask – administering gas, not repelling it – would evoke in later years) I was introduced to Mickey Mouse, I touched him. More than that, I looked out on a world of blitzed buildings and bomb shelters through his eyes. I *was* Mickey, a flesh-and-blood effigy of a celluloid figment.[2]

For grown-ups, too, Mickey was a cheering figure in those grim days. His perky image was painted on the fuselage of some American and British aeroplanes. One such emblem inspired the title of Len Deighton's 1982 novel *Goodbye, Mickey Mouse*, about American flyers stationed in Britain during World War II:

The aircraft smelled new with its mixture of leather, paint and high-octane fuel. On its nose a brightly painted Mickey Mouse danced ...
Earl Koenige's *Happy Daze* was nearest to Farebrother. There was a lightly clad girl and a bottle of whisky painted on its nose ... *Mickey Mouse II*, now turned away from him, featured the cartoon rodent toting six-guns and a ten-gallon hat.[3]

So while Mickey Mouse gas masks were protecting British civilians, Mickey Mouse planes were in action over Germany. And Walt Disney was very proud that the password of the Allied Forces on D-Day – 6 June 1944 – was "Mickey Mouse."

Hitler disapproved of Mickey and banned him in Germany about 1935. Perhaps those black ears did not strike Hitler as having the right Aryan antecedents. Mussolini, however, was a great Mickey fan,[4] and a framed photograph sent from him to Walt Disney is still kept at Disney Studios. When a number of Mickey drawings were shown in art galleries across America in 1933, *Screenland* gave the story this headline: "'I'm the Mous-solini of Geniuses,' Cries Modest Mickey as High Art Claims Him for Her Own."

Mickey Mouse had come into the world at a grim time, too – the eve of the Crash, in 1928. Edwin C. Hill wrote in the *Boston American* of 8 August 1933: "Perhaps Mickey's celebrity is not so amazing, after all, when one remembers that he came to us at the time the country needed him most – at the beginning of the Depression. He has helped us laugh away our troubles, forget our creditors and keep our chins up."

The *Albany (New York) News* of 24 October 1933 suggested that, "When the last plaintive moan of the depression has faded to a feeble whisper and the last tear is dried it might be well in order to give some thanks to a Mr. Walter Disney." Disney told the reporter he had chosen a mouse for his cartoons because he "wanted a little fellow." He added: "The public likes little fellows in comedy. They always get it in the neck because they are little. Everyone picks on them, and sympathy is thereby aroused. So when the little fellows finally triumph over their bigger aggressors, the public rejoices with them."

Arthur Millier, writing in the *Los Angeles Times* on 5 November 1933 offered a similar explanation of Mickey's popularity. To Millier, the Disney pictures were like the morality plays of the Middle Ages, being "cast in the simplest, most universally appealing dramatic form."

Mickey is "Everyman," battling for life and love against a devil who is both villain and chief comedian of the piece. He may be the big rough foreman of that grand cartoon, *Building a Building* (1933), who personifies lust and power and is so terrifyingly husky and ruthless that no little mouse would dare defy him – unless he possessed powers that can triumph over the forces of evil. Mickey has them. He is honest, decent, a good sportsman... Mickey has his little weaknesses but there is no question which side he is on. He is little David who slays Goliath. He is that most popular, because most universally conceivable hero – the little man who shuts his eyes and pastes the big bully in the jaw.

In *Mickey's Service Station* (1935), the last Mickey film to be made in black and white, Mickey and his pals are garage hands. They "overhaul" (but in fact wreck) the automobile of that perennial villain Peg Leg Pete – who plays the same bully role as Stromboli, the menacing puppeteer, has in *Pinocchio*. Mickey and his gang take the car to bits and reassemble it like an apple-pie bed (finding that a cricket is the cause of its maddening squeak). As Peg Leg Pete plumps himself aggressively behind the steering-wheel and tries to start the car, which promptly explodes, our sympathies are wholly with the browbeaten workers who thus get their revenge on the overbearing capitalist. It would not be too fanciful to interpret these seven minutes of fun as a miniature satire anticipating by 10 years the message of Orwell's *Animal Farm* (1945).

Disney's *Three Little Pigs* (1933) was a parable even closer to Orwell's novel, even though in the former the pigs are heroes, in the latter, villains. Its catchy theme song, "Who's Afraid of the Big Bad Wolf?" ousted "Brother, Can You Spare a Dime?" and symbolized the will of ordinary Americans not to truckle under. It became the unofficial anthem of the New Dealers.

Of course, political polemics were not Disney's motive in making the Mickey Mouse films or any others of his films. He was by no means a left-wing doctrinaire, and indeed, in the 1940s he gained a reputation as a union-basher. But he was a former farm boy and newspaper roundsman who had come up the hard way and had ended up, like Judy Garland as Dorothy in *The Wizard of Oz* (1939), a long way from Kansas City – where some of his childhood privations had been endured. As a child, Walt Disney was occasionally beaten by his father Elias, which may account for the violence to which some critics took exception in the early Mickey films, and perhaps also for the "spanking clock" in *Pinocchio*.

It seemed specially apt that Prohibition, the anti-drink legislation so closely associated with the Depression years, should end on Walt Disney's thirty-second birthday. The *New York Post* commented facetiously, on 5 December 1933: "It is the day on which we can all drink in celebration of Walt Disney's birthday. National prohibition repeal is merely incidental to this event, the opening of the liquor sluices having been thoughtfully arranged by a Mickey Mouse-conscious Government so that the two occasions could be made to coincide." Repeal brought a host of new cocktails, including a "New Deal" and, inevitably, a "Mickey Mouse."[5]

Not only did Mickey have the right attitude to encourage people to snap out of the Depression; he helped thousands of them to do so. He saved at least three companies from ruin. The Ingersoll Watch Company was just ticking over with 300 employees when the ingenious Mickey Mouse watch, with gloved "hands," was introduced in mid-1933. Within a few months, 3,000 people were on the payroll. By 1 June 1935 the company had sold 2½ million Mickey watches at $2.95 retail. In 1933 alone, some 900,000 were sold; and in a special promotion at Macy's department store in New York, over 11,000 were sold in a single day. By 1939 the Mickey Mouse watch was such a recognized part of American life that one was sealed in the World's Fair time-capsule buried in New York.

The Norwich Knitting Company in Norwich, New York, had shut down some of its textile mills when, in 1932, it signed a contract to manufacture Mickey Mouse sweaters. By 1933, three-quarters of the population of Norwich were being employed to make the sweaters. By 1935, over a million sweaters a year were being sold, and one-third of Norwich's population was making enough money in overtime alone to support its families.

Even more telling was the story of the Lionel Corporation. On 7 May 1934 it went into receivership with liquid assets of $62,000 and liabilities of $296,000. In February 1935, in the U.S. District Court at Newark, New Jersey, Judge Guy L. Fake lifted the corporation out of receivership. Mickey Mouse and Minnie, pumping a small handcar round a circular track, formed the toy that had "put the business back on its feet," the judge said. This was a slight exaggeration since, as Cecil Munsey has pointed

Walt Disney posed among some examples of the hundreds of different items of merchandise featuring Mickey Mouse that were manufactured during the 1930s.

out, the handcars accounted for only about 5 per cent of Lionel's business during that period.[6] Even so, since the summer of 1934 Lionel had sold 253,000 of the cars at $1 each; and through Mickey's association with Lionel, its other products suddenly became popular. This message was quickly exploited by Disney's trade representative, with a red and black advertisement captioned: "Red to Black on a Handcar — Mickey Mouse Pulls That Way."[7]

When there were still only five candles on Mickey's birthday cake, *Forbes* magazine, the hard-boiled bi-monthly of American business, devoted an article to his business acumen. By then some 40 manufacturers were licensed to use his name in making and selling novelties: the latest product was a Mickey radio. The importance of Mickey merchandise had been recognized in the appointment of Kay Kamen to handle licensing. Kamen was a

Kansas City advertising executive who had already had a success with a comic promotional figure called "Tim."

While it is not true that if you called up the Chock Full o' Nuts stores on the telephone a polite voice said "Nuts," it *is* true that if you telephoned BRyant 9-1990 in New York, a lady who had kept that schoolgirl inflection said "Mickey Mouse." Wags used to ring the number on rainy days just to hear her say it. BRyant 9-1990 was Kay Kamen's office number. "Mickey Mouse is better known than I am," he explained to a Boston reporter.[8]

On becoming Disney's licenser-in-chief, Kamen had arrived at three decisions. He would license only one manufacturer in each class; centralize in his office all advertising, packaging and promotion plans; and stipulate in licensing contracts the outlets through which Mickey Mouse merchandise could be retailed, or indeed re-tailed. Kamen maintained scrupulously high standards, turning down hundreds of applications for licenses from manufacturers he considered sub-standard. If he had not done so, Disney undoubtedly would have transferred the licensing powers to somebody else. It infuriated Disney to see a poor copy of Mickey. He did not much like, though he just tolerated, the version made by Dean's Rag Book Company in England, as the dolls had a "toothy sneer." (Bernard C. Shine has described the Dean's version of Pluto, with "beady bug eyes," as well as the sneer, as "kind of like Pluto with rabies."[9])

Disney ordered that Mickey should never be used to advertise cigarettes, beer, laxatives or other patent medicines. There was one humane exception to this rule. Though Mickey was not allowed to promote in the United States a Scott & Bowne cod liver oil product called Scott's Emulsion, Disney granted permission for him to recommend it in South America because of the high incidence of rickets there.[10]

But Disney was happy for Mickey to be incorporated into designs on belt buckles, porridge bowls, ice-cream cones, chewing-gum, dolls, hot-water bottles, paper decorations, paper masks, story books, jewelry, bath and lounging robes, women's dresses, cretonnes, chintzes and marquisettes, play and sun suits, caps, soaps and games. From this little mouse, what a mountain!

Children were naturally the main target of Kamen's marketing campaign – the same children who, from 1929 onwards, were joining Saturday noontime Mickey Mouse clubs at their local cinemas. (These clubs were at their height in 1932, with over a million members in America – more than the Boy Scouts and Girl Scouts of America combined.) The *Cleveland Plain Dealer* of 29 September 1935 suggested that a child who had been thoroughly "sold" on the Disney characters could spend a day well filled with their company, after this fashion:

In his room, bordered with M.M. wall paper and lighted with M.M. lamps, his M.M. alarm clock awakens him, providing his mother forgets! Jumping from his bed where his pajamas and the bedding are the M.M. brand, to a floor the rugs and linoleum upon which are M.M. sponsored, he puts on his M.M. moccasins and rushes to the bathroom to have the first chance at ... no, you're wrong ... at the soap made in the Disney manner, as are also his toothbrush, hair-brush and towels.
  Then, all dressed up, he goes down to breakfast ... his sweater, waist, tie, belt, socks and garters, handkerchief and watch all bear his favorite emblem, and for outdoors he has helmet, sweat-shirt, muffler and rubber boots with M.M. couchant and rampant. For his sister and younger brother there are rain-capes and umbrellas, metal and leather purses, jewelry, hair-ribbons and play togs equally covered by the merry mouse of the Disney atelier.
  At breakfast they eat an M.M. endorsed cereal and dairy products ... from china and silver in the well-known pattern. The jam with which they garnish their toast comes from a jar which, when emptied, becomes an M.M. bank.
  For school their pen, pencil, pencil box, painting set, writing tablet and lunch box are all decorated with their favorite's likenesses. And after school, in season, they can go fishing with their M.M. fishing kit or stay home and use a well labelled tool box. Or if they'd rather they can entertain themselves with their movie or talkie projector, or games, printing outfit, or books, football or basketball equipment.
  The younger children haven't been neglected for they've

spent the day with dolls, doll houses, toy furniture, toy dishes of china, aluminum tops, blocks, trains of many kinds, push and pull toys, wheelbarrows, wagons and velocipedes, all, I assure you, of the Mickey-Mouse brand.

By 1933, Mickey was replacing Santa Claus as a Christmas attraction at American stores. If there had been a Santas' Union, there would probably have been strikes and picketing. "For the first time in history, the venerable gentleman is truly left 'holding the sack'," the Boston *Christian Science Monitor* jested on 20 December 1933. The *Boston Herald* reported on the same day:

Through his spokesman John Mangum, who is Head Claus of the Association of S.C.'s, Santa has announced his displeasure with the competition which department stores are providing in the form of Mickey Mouse and the Three Little Pigs. These creatures, while doubtless possessed of a definite place in the hearts and affections of the young, have nothing to do with Christmas, Santa asserts. Therefore they must go...

But in some American cities, Santa was already capitulating. If he couldn't beat Mickey and Co., they would have to join him. The *Dayton (Ohio) News* of 27 November 1933 reported that "At the specific request of S. Claus himself, Rikes has obtained from Walt Disney, their noted creator, exclusive rights for participation in their Thanksgiving Day Toyland parade of not only Mickey Mouse, but all his friends and relatives." And that year Colonel Walter Merriam Pratt of Boston sent out invitations to a giant party in the form of legal summonses served by Mickey Mouse. Some of the invitees, Colonel Pratt told the *Boston Transcript*, had had their lawyers draw up replies. And one sent "a tremendous cheese" from Pierce's store.[11]
  In December 1933, an article on "Christmas at Loeser's" (Frederick Loeser & Co., Brooklyn, New York) in *Playthings* magazine, New York reported:

Mickey Mouse and his well-known friends predominate all the displays. The pillars are decorated with vari-colored pennants each with the figure of Mickey Mouse upon it. Cut-out wooden figures of Mickey and Minnie dominate the walls and the top of the display shelves... Once again Mickey Mouse plays a prominent part in that the surprise package feature is built around him. A "live" Mickey Mouse resides in Mickey Mouse Castle. The children produce a ticket at the entrance to the castle for twenty-five or fifty cents. This ticket entitles them to a present from Mickey Mouse...

In 1934, Goodyear – famous for its blimps – produced a 50-foot inflatable Mickey Mouse to lead the Macy's Thanksgiving Day Parade in New York. And for Christmas 1935, the Lionel Corporation issued a special version of the handcar which had pulled it out of the red. This was manned by a Santa Claus with a grinning, toy Mickey lolling contentedly in Santa's sack.

The Head Claus and his subordinate Clauses were not the only people to suffer from Mickey's popularity. The success of the animated Mickey Mouse cartoons meant the death of the old one- and two-reel custard-pie comedies. The Hollywood studios where the short comedies were filmed were closing down. "Even the beautiful Mack Sennett Studio at Studio City, northwest of Hollywood, is dark save for some rented space," the *New York Herald Tribune* mourned on 12 December 1933.

Like Santa Claus, Charlie Chaplin decided he had better ask Mickey to join him. The *Seattle (Washington) Motion Picture Record* of 28 February 1931 reported:

> Word has come that Charlie Chaplin has requested that his latest production, *City Lights*, be accompanied wherever possible with a Mickey Mouse cartoon. This unusual request bears upon Chaplin's high regard for the ... cartoon character and surety in that his own presentation will meet with a greater acclaim after an audience has been amused by Mickey's antics.

The *Portland (Oregon) News* of 16 March 1931 printed a cartoon by George Corley of Chaplin handing Mickey a bouquet. But by 1933, even Chaplin seemed in eclipse. In November 1930, George Davis wrote in the *Cleveland (Ohio) Press*, "Disney's cartoons are all the more welcome because

production of posed comics has become almost a lost art. Chaplin may be funny, still. No one knows. His pictures have been so few and far between since he made a fortune and began spending most of his time idling in Europe."

Hal Roach was still doing some short comedy business, but only because he had made, developed and retained the services of the ever-popular Laurel and Hardy. Like Mickey Mouse, Roach has proved a survivor: in December 1984 he attended the fiftieth anniversary celebrations for the Santa Anita Race Track, Arcadia, California, which he had helped to found in 1934.

The old-style one- and two-reel comedies had cost between $25,000 and $40,000. The average cost of a Mickey Mouse film was $18,000; of a Silly Symphony, about $20,000.[12] "Mickey Mouse is supreme," the *New York Herald Tribune* article of December 1933 concluded.

Mickey Mouse also benefited from the "purity" campaign which seized the movie industry in the 1930s. The "clean up the films" movement, in which the Roman Catholic Church was especially active, had begun several years before. And it had been given new momentum by three scandals. The first was the murder of the English director William Desmond Taylor, "an unsavory affair involving drugs, sexual perversion and two movie heroines, Mary Miles Minter and Mabel Normand."[13] The second was the arraignment of the comedian "Fatty" Arbuckle on a manslaughter charge (originally investigated as rape and murder). The third was the death in an asylum of the matinée idol and drug addict, Wallace Reid.

In 1921, when Will H. Hays had become the "Czar of Hollywood," president of the Motion Picture Producers and Distributors of America (M.P.P.D.A.), his first big fight had been to prevent the government intervening to impose censorship on films. He was successful. He was personally responsible for the overwhelming defeat of a film censorship bill before the Massachusetts state legislature. But, in return, he had to promise that the movie industry would purge itself.

In an early Hollywood press conference he proclaimed: "This industry must have towards that sacred thing, the mind of the

Bouquet for Mickey Mouse

No less a star than Charley Chaplin hands a floral tribute to Mickey Mouse. In releasing his new picture, "City Lights," now showing at the United Artists, Charley specified that a Mickey Mouse picture be shown on the same program with his picture. (Sketch by George Corley.)

The cartoon that appeared in the *Portland (Oregon) News* in March 1931 showing Charlie Chaplin offering a "floral tribute" to Mickey.

child, towards that clean virgin thing, that unmarked slate, the same responsibility, the same care about the impressions made upon it, that the best clergyman or the most inspired teacher of youth would have."[14] To that end the "Hays Formula" was introduced. Studios were to submit books, scripts and stories to the Hays Office before purchase. This did not satisfy the purity campaigners; and the coming of sound, with its new possibilities of verbal offence, gave urgency to the quest for a self-curbing system.

In 1929, Martin Quigley and Daniel A. Lord, S.J., both Roman Catholics, drew up the "Hays Office Code." This was adopted by the M.P.P.D.A. in 1930 and, in 1934, was made mandatory. Joseph I. Breen, also a Roman Catholic, was put in charge of the Production Code Administration, with power to withhold a certificate and Seal of Approval. Any company releasing a film without the Seal would be fined $25,000. The Code ruled that no picture should be produced "which will lower the moral standards of those who see it." There were particular requirements about sex, profanity, costume and "repellent subjects." One clause stipulated that "The treatment of bedrooms must be governed by good taste and delicacy."

The Catholic Church intended to make sure that the Code was sternly enforced. Already the National League of Decency had been formed, a Catholic censorship body which circulated classifications of films from "A1" (morally unobjectionable), to "C" (condemned).

On 23 April 1934, John Betjeman – the future Poet Laureate of Great Britain – who had been recently appointed film critic of the London *Evening Standard*, reported that "the Catholic Church in America has sent a questionnaire to every priest asking him details about his local cinema. It, too, wants to join in the 'clean up the films' game. This may be rather a blow for Mae West..." (In the same issue Betjeman wrote: "Silly Symphonies and Mickey Mouse are still, in spite of everything, the best entertainment the cinema provides.")

In the 1935 Jean Harlow film *Reckless*, Betjeman saw the deadening effects of the purity crusade: "It seemed to me that Jean Harlow herself had great cobras fascinating her, and she was unable to forget them and be her proper self. These cobras

Even Mickey Mouse fell foul of the censor during the mid-1930s, when the National League of Decency tried to impose high moral standards on the entire movie industry.

That little scoundrel, Mickey Mouse, has run afoul of scissor-wielding censors. His latest appearances have been handicapped by an avalanche of "Don'ts"

were the beetle-browed Puritan censors, watching every dress she wore and every remark and movement she made, waiting to strike."[15]

Mae West and Harlow might suffer from the purity movement; not so Mickey Mouse. Unlike the average sex-gangster-murder movies of the 1930s, Mickey Mouse films were fit for children, a "family audience." The same is still more true of animated cartoons today, when sex and violence in films have reached a pitch inconceivable in the 1930s. The re-issue of *Pinocchio*, in late 1984, was fourth in the Christmas box-office ratings, after *Beverly Hills Cop*, *Dune* and *City Heat*. The notion of pornographic

animated cartoons, realized in the 1970s in Ralph Bakshi's *Fritz the Cat* and *Heavy Traffic*, has not caught on.

But even Mickey did not altogether escape the censor's scissors. As early as July 1930 German censors banned *The Barnyard Battle* (1929) because "the wearing of German military helmets by an army of cats which opposes a militia of mice is offensive to the national dignity." Later in 1930, a Mickey film was banned in Ohio because a cow was shown reading a copy of Elinor Glyn's "scandalous" novel *Three Weeks*. And in February 1931 *Time* magazine reported:

Motion Picture Producers and Distributors of America last week announced that, because of the complaints of many censor boards, the famed udder of the cow in Mickey Mouse cartoons was now banned. Cows in Mickey Mouse or other cartoon pictures in the future will have small or invisible udders quite unlike the gargantuan organ whose antics of late have shocked some and convulsed other of Mickey Mouse's patrons. In a recent picture the udder, besides flying violently left and right or stretching far out behind when the cow was in motioned, heaved with its panting when the cow stood still; it also stretched, when seized, in an exaggerated way.

The *New York Herald* of 3 January 1931 ran the same story under the headline "They Shudder at an Udder."

But, in general, Mickey films were considered good clean fun. The press sheet *Columbia Pictures Presents Mickey Mouse* (1931) reassured theater managers that "Mickey, a moral young mouse, never sings in his bath-tub unless the more delicate portions of his sinuous torso are concealed by a flock of rich, creamy suds." But Bernard C. Shine has noted that "The shorts worn by Mickey were not worn because of any sense of modesty. If modesty were the motivation, one might ask why Donald Duck never wore pants (except, oddly enough, when swimming)! And if modesty were a concern, why was early Minnie usually topless?"

In October 1933, *The Herald*, Montreal, Quebec, reported a speech that Mrs. Alfred Zimmen had delivered to the Local Council of Women. "Except for the Mickey Mouse pictures the cinema was condemned as a narcotic with a stupefying effect on the people." Mrs. Zimmen had spoken darkly of "disguised immorality."

The whole concept of Mickey Mouse was one of child-like innocence. His essential character is that of a mischievous small boy. In March 1932, Walt Disney wrote an article in *American Cinematographer* about his own amateur shooting with a little Victor 16mm camera. "When I bought my camera," he wrote, "I intended to use it entirely for my own pleasure. But Mickey Mouse intervened. He always does! Ever since I first drew him, he has become more and more real, and *like a real child*,* ingratiating by demanding more and more of my spare time." The official instructions for Disney artists written by Fred Moore suggest that:

Mickey seems to be the average young boy of no particular age; living in a small town, clean living, fun loving, bashful around girls, polite and as clever as he must be for the particular story.

In some pictures he has a touch of Fred Astaire; in others of Charlie Chaplin, and some of Douglas Fairbanks, but in all of these there should be some of the young boy.

As usual, Disney showed an instinct for popular taste. The animal behaviorist Konrad Lorenz has pointed out that humans feel affection for animals with juvenile features – bulging craniums, large eyes, retreating chins and a "springy elastic consistency."[16] Animals with small eyes and long snouts do not elicit the same response.

Mickey's childishness appeals to the child-loving element in our subconscious, evoking "an automatic surge of disarming tenderness." One might compare Mickey with Peter Pan, in that he never grows up; or with Alice in Wonderland in his bemused response to the oddities he finds in the world. And it is significant that Disney made "Alice" films even before his first Mickey cartoon, as well as the full-scale *Alice* of 1951. But perhaps the previous literary character with whom Mickey has most in common is Voltaire's Candide, with his boundless optimism and his conviction that all's for the best in the best of all possible worlds. Walt Disney wrote of Mickey in *Overland Monthly* (October 1933):

We see to it that nothing ever happens that will cure his faith in the transcendent destiny of ... Mickey Mouse, or his conviction that the world is just a big apple pie. When on occasions, *as boys will*,* the lad becomes too cocky and struts vaingloriously before admiring Minnie, Fate in the gag department kicks him from the rear and rolls him ignobly in the dust of gentle ridicule... Sex is not of interest to Mickey: the story of the travelling salesman is of no more interest than the ladies lingerie department. He is not a little mouse. He only looks like one. He is Youth, the Great Unlicked and Uncontaminated.

If Mickey is not a mouse but only looks like one, why did Disney choose that guise for him? Disney's account of the genesis of Mickey changed with every interview he gave. I do not mean to suggest that Disney was a pathological liar (though over-strictness such as Elias Disney visited on his son can school a child to tell lies – to avoid punishment – rather than achieve its objective of persuading him to tell the truth). Disney was a showman dedicated to giving the public what it wanted. Journalists wanted a good story, and he would give them one.

"I first got the idea, I suppose," he told the *Minneapolis Star* (6 August 1933), "When I was working in an office in Kansas City. The girls used to put their lunches in wire waste baskets and every day the mice would scamper around in them after crumbs. I got interested and began collecting a family in an old box. They became very tame and by the time I was ready to turn them loose they were so friendly they just sat there on the floor looking at me. I had to shoo them away."

"There was a live Mickey and a live Minnie scampering over Walt Disney's drawing board as the young artist dreamed his dreams," the *Boston American* recorded on 8 August 1933, "for there were two mice that played about in Walt's room and which he tamed and taught to pose for him." The writer described how Disney had lured the mice to his drawing board "with a trail of crumbs and cheese."

*Author's italics.

By November 1933, when *Psychology* published an article on Disney by "G.M.K.," the story had become a little more elaborate. "G.M.K." claimed that with a few dollars gained by drawing pictures for a barber in Kansas City, Disney had rigged up a "smelly garage" as a studio.

There he made the acquaintance of Mickey. One evening as he was bending over his drawing board, two little mice scampered across his table. Amused at their capers, he began to make friends with them. And presently they were serving as his models. For hours they would sit on his drawing board, while he worked, combing their whiskers and licking their chops in true mouse fashion. And Walt would weave them into human situations and make them tell funny human stories.

But the *Columbia (S.C.) Record* of 11 November 1933 carried a quite different story. Disney told them that Charlie Chaplin had been the inspiration for Mickey.

I can't say just how the idea came. We wanted another animal. We had a cat, so naturally a mouse came to mind. We felt that the public, and especially the children, like animals that are cute and little. I think that we are rather indebted to Charlie Chaplin for the idea. We wanted something appealing, and we thought of a tiny bit of a mouse that would have something of the wistfulness of Chaplin – a little fellow trying to do the best he could.

Disney added that when a rough cat villain was needed it was based on Wallace Beery; and when a polished cat villain was needed, the artists thought of Erich von Stroheim. The analogy between Mickey and Charlie Chaplin was often made. John C. Moffitt described Disney's characters in the *Providence (R.I.) Bulletin* of 4 April 1934 as "these Chaplins from the ink bottle." And the cartoonist Alain, in the *New Yorker* of 20 January 1934 showed a group of sophisticates in a streamlined interior. A young man on a chromium-plated stool is expostulating to a lank-haired girl: "All you hear is Mickey Mouse, Mickey Mouse,

Mickey Mouse! It's as though Chaplin had never lived!"

The *Bismarck Hotel (Chicago) Magazine* of December 1933 carried a profile of Disney by Bill Harshe, who wrote: "He has had personal contact with many mice. Working late in a Kansas City, Missouri, cartoonist's office he occasionally dozed off and awoke to find them scurrying in and out of the wire mesh of the waste-paper basket where he had thrown his lunch box." And Harshe quoted Disney as saying of mice: "Their hands are like humans ... They only live in dark places because they are driven to it, fugitives from the brooms of intolerant janitors."

A new angle on the story appeared in the *Athens (Ga) Banner-Herald* of 26 December 1933. The Chicago Art Institute, which was then holding an exhibition of original Disney cartoons, had released this story of Mickey's origins in its weekly letter to the Press:

It was Disney's brother's daughter, aged six, who was chiefly responsible for "Mickey" ... Six years ago Disney had a 5-dollar a month studio over a garage where he sat at night and watched the antics of a pair of mice. After weeks of patient persuasion, he tamed them so that they would climb upon his drawing board. There they sat up and nibbled bits of cheese in their paws or even ate from his hand. As he watched them, he occasionally wrote letters to his niece. The letters described the activities of the mice and sometimes were illustrated with drawings of them doing funny, fantastic human things.

The most embellished treatment of the mouse-model legend was by John C. Moffitt in his April 1934 article in the *Providence Bulletin*.

The original Mickey ... probably has long since perished ignobly in the mousetrap of some annoyed housewife who did not realise that it was a celebrity that had been getting into the cheese...
    Disney had found the little fellow and several of his companions in his desk at a studio where the artist was employed to make ad-films. The original Mickey, with Minnie

and several other relations, had been induced to enter the studio not as models but as samplers of the luncheons of the artists. If they didn't like the pie they ate the erasers. They sharpened their teeth on the pencils.

Although he is no lover of mice, Walter Disney is a farm boy who dislikes the thought of animals suffering. He wouldn't let his companions buy a trap that would mangle the intruders. After some days' shopping he found an elaborate affair that took mice alive. The mice lost no time in getting themselves caught in Walt's fancy trap. Walt had planned to drown them, but when he saw them he made them prisoner in the waste basket with a piece of screen over it. He gave them odd drawings to make a nest of and he took to carrying two luncheons, one for himself and one for the mice.

When he moved out of the ad-film studio to start a shop of his own the mice went with him. One of them had become so tame that Walt would take him out and let him run around the edge of his drawing board. Walt got very fond of him.

He did not part with the friendly mice until he set out for California. "I took the waste basket full of mice to a vacant lot," Walt says, "and turned them loose. The family all ran into the weeds, but the clown mouse that had played on the drawing board didn't seem to want to go. He stood around looking at me. I had to stamp my foot on the pavement and yell at him to make him beat it. That's the last I ever saw of him."

Moffitt added defensively: "A magazine writer recently dismissed the story of the mouse which inspired Mickey as a myth. But Walt Disney spent one whole morning telling it to me and he insisted it was true."

The magazine which had dismissed the story of mice models was the February 1934 issue of *Cosmopolitan*: "Fiction has it that a mouse roamed Walt's workroom; that the two became friendly, and the Mickey Mouse character originated in this [Kansas City] room. It is a nice story, but false. As a matter of fact, Mickey Mouse's papa is not overly fond of mice. He jumps out of their way, and doesn't go looking for them."

The truth, less flattering to Disney than his portrayal as the St Francis of Assisi of mice, seems to be that he had failed to read the small print of the contract he had signed with Charles Mintz concerning rights to the name of the cartoon character Oswald the Lucky Rabbit. The contract in fact gave Mintz control. In 1928, as Disney was returning to California from New York by train after making this depressing discovery, he tried to think of a cartoon character who would be similar enough to Oswald to share his popularity without infringing Mintz's copyright. The answer was a mouse, who like Oswald would have big ears, a happy grin, bendy limbs and a pair of shorts with big, useless buttons. Disney wanted to call him "Mortimer Mouse." His young wife, Lillian, thought that was too pompous and suggested "Mickey." Mrs. Disney's feeling for popular taste was not infallible: six years later, she was quite sure that Donald Duck was going to be a flop. But in christening Mickey she helped to make her husband a multi-millionaire. By removing Mickey from the snooty Mortimers, Marmadukes, Montmorencys and other upper-drawer rodents, she made him accessible and acceptable to a mass market. (Mortimer Mouse was not lost to history, however. In 1936, he took the title role in the film *Mickey's Rival*, as a competing suitor for Minnie's hand.)

It is only right to mention that in his book *The Art of Walt Disney* (1973), Christopher Finch cast some doubt on the story that Disney "conceived Mickey on the train, returning to Hollywood from his angry encounter with Mintz." Over the years, Finch wrote, this story "became so polished by repetition that it began to lose its sense of reality and to take on the character of an official myth." One begins to treat the whole saga – or series of sagas – as a shaggy mouse story.

In whatever way he was conceived, Mickey was "born" in the same year as Shirley Temple. But he was as different from that ringletted prodigy as the suburban Rupert Bear was different from A.A. Milne's Pooh, the darling of the British upper-middle class. Mickey's demotic appeal was all the more advantageous in the Depression years that were supervening. At the time of Mickey's fiftieth birthday in 1978, Maurice Sendak – himself a great fantasy artist, children's book illustrator and collector of Mickey memorabilia – recalled what it had meant to him, as a poor Brooklyn boy, to grow up with Mickey Mouse:

Those were the Depression years and we had to make do. Making do – for kids, at least – was mostly a matter of comic books and movies. Mickey Mouse, unlike the great gaggle of child movie stars of that period, did not make me feel inferior. Perhaps it was typical for kids of my generation to suffer badly from unthinking parental comparisons with the then-famous silver-screen moppets. There is no forgetting the cheated, missed-luck look in my father's eyes as he turned from the radiant image of Shirley Temple back to the three ungolden children he'd begotten. Ah, the wonderful, rich, American-dream blessing of having a Shirley Temple girl and a Bobby Breen boy! I never forgave those yodelling, tap-dancing, brimming-with-glittering-life miniature monsters.

But Mickey Mouse had nothing to do with any of them. He was our common street friend. My brother and sister and I chewed his gum, brushed our teeth with his toothbrush ... and read about his adventures in comic strips and story books.[18]

But if Mickey appealed to kids in the lower reaches of American society, he was at the same time appealing to the mandarins of the art world – and to the arbiters of "Society," too. The *Evansville (Ind.) Press* of 8 December 1933 reported that "The Art of Mickey Mouse," an exhbition of Disney's work, would be on display at the Temple of the Fine Arts early in January."

Mickey Mouse drawings had first been exhibited in public at the Kennedy Galleries, New York, in the summer of 1932. The show was such a big success that it ran for six weeks instead of the two weeks originally planned. "Galleries Request Disney Drawings," a headline in the *Toledo (Ohio) Blade* of 11 December 1933 announced. A demand by art galleries in all parts of the country for the exhibition of the original Mickey Mouse and Silly Symphony drawings had made it necessary for the College Art Association, which was organizing the drawings' tour, to revise its schedule to meet the many requests.

On 14 December 1933 the *Burlington (N.C.) Times-News* published a story with a Chicago dateline: "The antics of Mickey Mouse ... ascended to the stately walls of the Chicago Art Museum for the winter exhibits of the Art Institute." The article compared Mickey's antics favourably with the "grim Russian morbidities of Boris Grigoriev" (the Russian *salon* artist).

In 1934 Walt Disney was elected an honorary member of the British Art Workers' Guild of which Sir Edwin Lutyens, George Bernard Shaw and the poet Laurence Binyon were then members. In 1935, an exhibition of Disney art was staged in the Leicester Galleries, London, which more customarily showed Picasso, Epstein and Walter Sickert. Between 1938 and 1939 an exhibition of Mickey Mouse and other Disney art toured the United States. It was seen by some five million people in 38 museums, 14 universities and 53 art galleries.

One might think that the art world showed rare percipience by elevating Mickey to the status of gallery art at such an early stage. After all, it still seemed revolutionary in the 1960s for Roy Lichtenstein to paint large-scale comic strip frames and exhibit them. But Mickey's precocious appearance in the galleries is not really so surprising. The Cubists had prepared the way for him. Culture shock-absorbers were already in place. Picasso may seem an unlikely herald for Mickey Mouse, but once the principles of Cubism were accepted, it did not need a vast shift of perspective to accept what might be called "Circle-ism." For it was on the circle that Mickey was based.

"I evolved him originally out of circles, they were simple and easy to handle," Disney told the *Minneapolis Star* of 6 August 1933. Mickey was composed of three circles of equal size, balanced on top of each other like some primitive idol of balancing dolmen-stones. The head was one circle, the body was another, and the bandy legs were contained within the third. The Studio's instructions to artists suggested that the ears should be "not-quite" circles.

Those ears and their unnatural placement – always seen in profile no matter what stance Mickey adopts – embody an art principle that Professor Sir Ernst Gombrich has noted as characteristic of the ancient Egyptians. He wrote of the Egyptians that "They did not set out to sketch nature as it appeared to them from any fortuitous angle. They drew from memory, according to strict rules which ensured that everything that had to go into the picture would stand out in perfect clarity."[19] This was also Disney's objective. Their method, Gombrich suggested, resembled that of the map-maker rather than that of the painter.

He gave as an example the painting of a pond from a tomb in Thebes (*c.*1400 B.C.) in the British Museum.

> If we had to draw such a motif we might wonder from which angle to approach it. The shape and character of the trees could be seen clearly only from the sides, the shape of the pond would be visible only if seen from above. The Egyptians had no compunction about this problem. They would simply draw the pond as if it were seen from above, and the trees from the side. The fishes and birds in the pond, on the other hand, would hardly look recognizable as seen from above, so they were drawn in profile.[20]

As Gombrich pointed out, children often draw by a similar method; but they are less consistent than the ancient Egyptians. With the Egyptian artists, everything had to be represented from its most characteristic angle. Gombrich described the effect this had on the representation of the human body:

> The head was most easily seen in profile so they drew it sideways. But if we think of the human eye we think of it as seen from the front. Accordingly, a full-face eye was planted into the side view of the face. The top half of the body, the shoulders and chest, are best seen from the front, for then we see how the arms are hinged to the body. But arms and legs in movement are much more clearly seen sideways... The Egyptian artists found it hard to visualize either foot seen from the outside. The preferred the clear outline from the big toe upwards. So both feet are seen from the inside, and the man on the relief [a tomb portrait of Hesire, *c.*2700 B.C.] looks as if he had two left feet.[21]

Mickey Mouse is drawn on the same principle. Except when shown absolutely head-on and full-face, he looks as if he has two left ears (or two right ears, according to which side of his head is shown). Walt Disney was delighted, as it happens, when an Egyptologist claimed to have discovered, in 1934, that "Mickey existed 2,000 years ago." But what suggested Mickey's side-by-side ears to Disney was not a bas-relief from ancient Egypt but the silhouette of the early cine-camera. It was natural that this most familiar of Hollywood images should be conscripted: it had a pointed "nose" and two "ears" in parallel. Picasso did something very similar when he joined together two bronze models of automobiles to form a "monkey."

Not everybody was happy to see Mickey received into the art world. A grumpy editorial in the *Columbus (Ohio) Dispatch* of December 16, 1933 commented, "We, for one, are sorry to see Mickey Mouse elevated to the plane of art. Once he was amusing. Now he is *significant* and at the mercy of every high-browed critic in the nation." There were analogous complaints about the way Disney, as some critics alleged, seemed to be abandoning the robust slapstick of Mickey for the more "arty" and sometimes embarrassingly coy fantasies of the Silly Symphonies. Joseph C. Furnas complained in the *New York Herald Tribune* of 3 December 1933 that a "nursery prettiness" had crept into Disney's work.

> *Lullaby Land* displays it in routine form... Babies rocked to sleep on tree-tops with dulcet feminine voices singing the appropriate song off-screen and the dainty agitation of the Three Little Pigs, quite in keeping with the pastel tones of the coloring... do not belong in the same country with the sardonic and violent happenings depicted in slashing black and white, which make up the life and times of Mickey Mouse. It appears disquietingly true that, in experimenting with his medium, Mr. Disney is getting a trifle too close to the soprano register.

Since color had been introduced, Furnas added, the temptation had been to please rather than to amuse, "to feed the audience spun sugar instead of knockout drops." The animated cartoon was being emasculated, he thought. Furnas missed the "loony improvisation" and "grand rowdiness" of the Mickey Mouse films. Mickey was being taken up by the intellectuals: was he now to be eclipsed by the cotton candy (candyfloss) characters of the Silly Symphonies?

There were even rumors that Disney was planning to phase Mickey out of movies and cage him in strip cartoons for the rest of his natural life. The *New York Sun* voiced them in 1934:

Consider the evidence. Look at the recent Mickey Mouse cartoons and see how they are failing in invention beside the increasing richness and fertility of the symphonies. Mickey is too valuable a trade-mark – has too many sidelines, too many gadgets – for Disney to be allowed to dispense with him altogether. But there seems to be a reasonable case for thinking that Mickey, the barnyard mouse, the sweetheart of Minnie, is becoming more and more a figure of the newspaper strip cartoon, while Disney himself is concentrating all his screen invention on the more impersonal and far wider field of the Silly Symphonies.

It was not true, of course. Disney had plenty of plans for Mickey movies. The possibilities were limitless. The animated cartoon lent itself to Surrealism as well as to Cubism. Salvador Dali himself worked at the Disney Studio for several months in 1946 working on a project that came to nothing – one of the great unconsummated marriages of history. Special effects could be achieved in this medium that would cause insuperable problems for the maker of films with flesh-and-blood actors.

In January 1934, the English novelist E.M. Forster contributed an article on "Mickey and Minnie" to *The Spectator* (London). He suggested that in a film to be called *Plastic Pools* – the Hockneyesque title was Forster's own contribution – Mickey should produce the audience for the next Silly Symphony as well as the film. "More would be spouted about than smoke. Siphons that pour zig-zag chocolates exploding into fleas – there are rich possibilities in the refreshments alone...."

In the same year, Fox Studios were racking their brains for answers to the following problems, in making a film of Dante's *Inferno*:

● How to create a storm of fire and brimstone. (A shower of petrol would not work. It only fell in sheets of flame. Small inflammable pellets, encased in drops of liquid, were used instead.)

● How to convey the illusion of nude transparent beings. (An X-ray photographic process was used.)

● How to make a lake of ice; a sea of boiling pitch; clothes that would be for ever in flame and yet not harm their wearers.

Not to mention Alexander cutting the Gordian knot and Medusa with her *coiffure* of writhing snakes.[22]

In animated cartoons, these effects were just as easy to achieve as a mouse blowing his nose on a polka-dot bandanna handkerchief. Mountains could be moved, camels swallowed. For once James Thurber may not have had his tongue entirely in his cheek when he suggested in *The Nation* of March 1934 that Disney should make an animated cartoon of *The Odyssey*. "Picture Mr. Disney's version of the overcoming of the giant, the escape tied to the sheep, the rage of Polyphemus as he hurls the tops of mountains at the fleeing ship of Ulysses and his men!" Some of Mickey Mouse's surreal exploits were more extreme than those. In *The Jazz Fool* (1929) a piano chases him. In *The Band Concert* (1935) – the film Toscanini enjoyed so much – a cyclone flings the band to pieces and flings them together again. "Mickey Mouse lives in a world in which space, time and the laws of physics are null," *Time* magazine suggested in 1931. "He can reach inside a bull's mouth, pull out his teeth and use them for castanets."[23]

Having derived something from Cubism and contributed something to Surrealism, in the 1960s Mickey became a prime ingredient in Pop Art. To the artists who were finding their inspiration in the everyday artefacts of popular culture – sometimes frankly *kitsch* or *schlock* – Mickey was an irresistible fetish-object. He was more interesting than a Heinz ketchup bottle or a Campbell's soup can, respectively immortalized by Michael English and Andy Warhol. He was *the* Pop icon. Indeed, in that he was early exhibited in art galleries, he might be considered the earliest manifestation of Pop Art, some 30 years before the allegedly pioneer works of Peter Blake and Richard Hamilton in England – the first example of an image plucked out of popular culture and enshrined in a gallery.

Claes Oldenburg was the Pop artist to whom Mickey meant most. As early as 1960, Oldenburg executed an oil wash on cardboard called "Empire Sign – with M and I Deleted." Of this, Gene Baro, in a standard work on the artist, has written, "The shape seems both phallic and a forerunner of the Mickey Mouse variations."[24]

In 1963 Oldenburg introduced Mickey directly into a poster advertising an exhibition of his own art at the Dwan Gallery, Los Angeles.[25] Of this design, showing Mickey with a red heart, Oldenburg commented: "The mouse is not only Mickey Mouse, but an amalgam — the legion of American movie mouse heroes."[26] (One suspects that this may have been a disingenuous disclaimer intended to deflect any attempt by the ever-vigilant Disney Studio to accuse Oldenburg of breach of copyright.) Oldenburg's future use of Mickey in his art so distorted Disney's creation that there could be no question of direct plagiarism, though Oldenburg candidly admitted the inspiration he had drawn from Mickey.

Oldenburg's large *Geometric Mouse* sculpture (1969), was based on Mickey's silhouette. The ground-plan of his ingenious *Mouse Museum* was "a combination of the early film camera and a stereotypical cartoon mouse," as the 1979 catalogue of the exhibition at the Museum Ludwig, Cologne, pointed out.[27] The origin of the *Mouse Museum* idea seems to have been the performance *Moveyhouse* sponsored by the Film-makers' Cinematheque at the 41st Street Theater, New York, in 1965. The players wore mouse masks.[28] In 1966, Oldenburg made drawings for a museum of popular art in the shape of a geometrical mouse.[29] In the same year he used the mouse shape as the letterhead of stationery printed for his first retrospective exhibition, at Moderna Museet in Stockholm. Oldenburg called the image "Strange Mickey Mouse." "The image is appropriate," explains the Cologne catalogue, "because in Swedish the word for mouse, *mus*, is similar to the word for museum, *museet*. Oldenburg's play with these words and the Swedish name for Mickey Mouse, *Musse Pigg*, anticipates the title *Mouse Museum*."[30] In 1969, Oldenburg made the first large version of the mouse in metal, which he titled *Geometric Mouse*. In 1972, he was given the chance to build the Mouse Museum, in the Neue Galerie, Kassel. The Mouse Museum was again constructed in the Museum of Contemporary Art, Chicago, in 1977 and filled with Oldenburg-selected objects such as a plastic hyacinth from Holland.[31]

Mickey was also, as an authentically Art Deco product, part of the nostalgia craze of the late 1960s and the 1970s. It was at this time that collecting Mickeyana spread from a few avant-garde devotees who found their Mickey watches and other relics in thrift shops and at swap-meets, to the rich and fashionable. For some collectors the passion for Mickey Mouse memorabilia is insatiable, beyond reason.

Bernard Shine, an American lawyer who has one of the finest collections of Mickey memorabilia, has analysed the different breeds of Mickey collectors, from the hermit who surrounds himself with Mickeys as an insulation from the rest of the world, to the "Born-Again Mouseketeer" who may, Shine speculates, have been a mouse in a previous life, and the "Mouse Junkie" or incurable addict.[32]

To such collectors as Shine, only the first decade of Mickey Mouse memorabilia merits consideration. The Mickeys they seek are those with "pie-eyes," so called because they resemble black pies with a slice missing. (In 1938 Mickey was given eyeballs in large white ovals so he could look from side to side.)

Another leading collector, Mel Birnkrant, deplores the way Mickey was later given "cute puffy cheeks so that his once geometrically pure, round head became an amorphous blob."[33] Birnkrant thinks it was a mistake for Disney to make Mickey look more real.[34] These collectors go for the early, rat-like Mickey dolls. Many were made in Nuremberg, traditionally the leading toy-making centre of Europe.

The finest dolls of all were made by the German manufacturer, Margarete Steiff. Between 1931 and 1934 her firm exported what Bernard Shine considers "the most magnificent Mickey and Minnie dolls ever to be produced."[35] They were even better than the Disney-approved dolls made in California by Charlotte Clark. Shine likes the Bavarian Chinaware imported from 1932 to 1934 by the Schumann Brothers of New York, decorated with pictures of Mickey and Minnie. A handsome series of German pot metal Mickey figurines was also made in the 1930s.

German folk tradition figured large in Disney's upbringing. His mother was of German descent. He was brought up on Grimms' *Fairy Tales*, from which the story of Snow White (which became a Disney film in 1937) was drawn. In his pre-Mickey days, Disney made a "Laugh-O-Gram" cartoon titled *The Four Musicians of Bremen* (1922). And in 1933, he made a Silly Symphony of *The Pied Piper*, that rat-infested legend that had been turned into a story by Goethe long before it was a poem by Robert Browning. Early Mickey has a rat's back-to-the-wall combativeness, even savagery, rather than a mouse's meekness and cuteness.

So Mickey may well have European, as well as American, antecedents; but then, his internationalism has never been in doubt. In France, he became Michel Souris; in Germany (before Hitler outlawed him), Micky Maus; in Spain, El Raton Miki; in Italy, Topolino; in Greece, Mikel Mus; in Sweden, Musse Pigg; in Brazil, Comondongo Mickey; in Central America, El Raton Miguelito; and in Japan, Miki Kuchi. In his infancy he was more popular in England and France than in America. As early as 1930, his effigy in wax, playing the piano in *The Opry House* (1929), went on show at Madame Tussaud's in London.

Queen Mary of England was a Mickey fan. Even though she was late for tea at the Palace, she refused to leave a theatre until she had seen the latest Mickey cartoon. In 1931, when the present Queen was Princess Elizabeth and five years old, Disney had a Christmas card specially engraved for her and hand-illuminated with a Mickey Mouse dressed as Santa, producing a miniature Mickey from his sack.

In the same year, *Time* magazine of 16 February said of Mickey Mouse: "Although his Christian name might be understood as an affront to Irish dignity, he has been respectfully reviewed in the *Irish Statesman* by Poet-Painter George ('A.E.') Russell." And the *New York Herald Tribune* of 8 March carried a photograph captioned, "A Film Character Invades the Latin Quarter: Left, Mickey Mouse and Felix cat appear on the smocks of art students in Paris, holding their annual Mardi Gras parade and celebration."

In 1933, Charles Lindbergh was one of the best known men in the world, partly because of his aeronautical exploits, but also because of the tragic kidnapping and killing of his baby in 1932. But when Lindbergh and his wife were forced to bring down their plane off Santona, north Spain, in November 1933, the couple were stopped by a Spanish customs official. The name Lindbergh was unknown to him so he would not allow them

ashore. "I know the Mickey Mouse and the Mae West," he said, "but not the Lindbergh."[36] Ironically, the first Mickey Mouse cartoon film made, *Plane Crazy* (1928), had been a parody of Lindbergh's adventures.

It was also in 1933 that Mahomet Zahir Khan, ruler of Hyderabad in south central India, declared Mickey Mouse the most popular of all movie stars among his people. And in December of that year Walt Disney received from Enrique C. Niese, the Argentine Consul in Los Angeles, a scroll from the National Academy of Fine Arts of Buenos Aires for his creation of Mickey.[37] In 1934, an entry on "Mickey Mouse" appeared in the new edition of the *Encyclopaedia Britannica*.

In 1935, the Soviet Government presented Disney with an antique, Russian cut-glass bowl, bestowed by the First Soviet Cinema Festival. Comrade Boris Shumiatsky, director-general of the Cinematography Institute of the U.S.S.R., told an American reporter that the Russian people would have no interest in Mae West, but that Mickey was "of cosmic value."[38] And Sergei Eisenstein, the Russian director of *The Battleship Potemkin*, said that Mickey was "America's one and only contribution to world culture."[39]

The Russians bought three Disney films, which became *Mikki Maus*, *Strannie Pinguini* and *Tri Malenkie Svinki*. Shumiatsky explained: "Disney is really showing us the people of the capitalistic world under the masks of pigs, mice and penguins: a definite social satire." The Russians tried to popularize their own animated cartoon character, a lovable little porcupine called Yozsh, but somehow he never caught on like Mickey, in Russia or anywhere else.[40]

Also in 1935 the 10-ten-year-old King of Siam, then at school in Lausanne, Switzerland, accepted from Disney the gift of several Mickey Mouse picture books. His attaché's office replied: "As you have correctly felt, His Majesty is interested in everything connected with Mickey Mouse, and His Majesty has read the books with great delight." Siam did not forget Disney's kindness. In 1960, as King of Thailand, Bhumibol Adulyadej conferred on him the Most Noble Order of the Crown.

In 1935, a Mickey cartoon strip serial began appearing daily in the *Peking Daily Times*. Also in that year a Mickey film was alleged to have cured a cripple in Murray Bay, Quebec. Convulsed with laughter throughout the performance, the invalid left his crutches in his cinema seat and staggered out, still laughing.

On 23 June 1935 the *New York Herald Tribune* carried a photograph captioned: "*Faust* competes with Mickey Mouse in Addis Ababa." It showed a street scene in the capital of Ethiopia, with bare-footed natives contemplating posters for both attractions. The same year, an admirer in Australia shipped a couple of live kangaroos to Disney. These gave him the idea for *Mickey's Kangaroo* (1935).

In *The Princess Comes Across* (1935), Carole Lombard, impersonating a Swedish noblewoman, informed interviewers that her favorite movie actor was "Meeky Moose." That might not sound so extraordinary, but that Lombard worked for Paramount and Mickey Mouse was distributed by the United Artists studio. Mickey no longer belonged just to the United States or to Walt Disney. He belonged to the world. In 1934 Harold Butcher, the New York correspondent of the London *Daily Herald*, had written in the *New York Times* of 28 October: "After a quick trip round the world – covering 20,000 miles at least – I have returned to New York to say that Mickey Mouse has been with me most of the time. On the Pacific, in Japan and China, at Manchouli – suspended precariously between Siberia and Manchuko – and in England." Butcher had been especially impressed with Mickey's popularity in Japan:

In theatre after theatre in Tokyo Mickey appears. It is fascinating to see his familiar outline on the billboards surrounded by intricate designs which might have been made by an artistic fly – designs mysterious to us but not to the Japanese who go to the box office to spend their yens and sens for a sight of Mickey.

I strolled along the Ginza, Tokyo's bazaar street, where the sidewalks are lined with stalls... Here you buy toys as cleverly conceived and executed as anything from Germany, home of toys. And here the Japanese buy models of Mickey Mouse. The foreigners buy Japanese dolls; the Japanese buy Mickey.

On a crowded railroad station walked a Japanese woman.

As conservative as Japan could make her in her dress – kimono, obi, getas. It was a hot day and she was using her fan. Suddenly I took a lively interest in that fan. It was a Mickey Mouse fan. There he was, the lad himself.

It had been even more of a surprise to Butcher to find Mickey and Minnie in Manchouli, the transfer station from the Chinese Eastern Railway to the Trans-Siberian. Butcher had had time to kill before the train started and had taken a walk. Suddenly he was confronted by Mickey and Minnie, "as large as life and twice as natural, looking at me from a store window."

It is said that wherever you go in the world, if you show people a picture of Mickey Mouse, you will get a smile. John Culhane, who was master-of-ceremonies for the Mickey Mouse fiftieth birthday celebrations at the Library of Congress, Washington D.C., wrote:

In the late Fifties, Dr. Tom Dooley, the "jungle doctor" and founder of Medico, was running a hospital ship off the coast of Southeast Asia that provided free medical care for whoever would come out of the jungle to his clinic. "Dooley had a problem getting children," recalled John Hench, an artist who is one of the key figures in the ongoing design of Disneyland and Disney World. "He wanted to know if he could use our characters – Mickey particularly... Dooley didn't understand what was going wrong at the time, but he knew from the experience he'd had that the Red Cross didn't work well – so he put Mickey on the side of his ship. Suddenly, kids who had refused to come out of the bush happily stood in line for medical examination. Obviously, hardly any of them had ever seen a picture of Mickey. But they recognized something. It wasn't the cartoon character, it was the symbol..."[42]

As an emblem, Mickey has had a potency somewhere between that of the swastika and the Coca-Cola logo in the hierarchy of 20th-century image-making. Human communication progressed from picture to emblem (pictogram) to language. In his short life, Mickey has made both transitions in fast motion. Today the words "Mickey Mouse" are used as an adjective, as in "Even a

Mickey Mouse tennis tournament like this oughta have a prize," or, less commonly, as a verb: "Don't you try to Mickey Mouse me!" Mickey fans should not be shocked or upset at the pejorative sense of these usages. Many swear-words, after all, invoke the most revered names ("Goddammit!" or the English cockney "Strewth!", a corruption of "God's Truth!"), and somebody who exclaims "Jesus Christ!" is rarely expressing unqualified delight. The disparaging or derogatory use of Mickey's name does not show any lack of love for him. Rather, it shows his acceptance as a key figure in 20th-century mythology – almost his apotheosis. He is a god over whom no religious wars have been fought, a myth that no one has wanted to explode.

Footnotes

1. Ronald Blythe, "Not by rations alone," *The Listener,* July 10, 1975, p.59.
2. Mr. M. J. R. Allen of the Department of Exhibits and Firearms, Imperial War Museum, London, confirms that the gas mask officially termed the "Small Child's Respirator" bore the nickname "the Mickey Mouse gas mask." (Letter of January 22, 1985). It has to be admitted that the so-called "Mickey Mouse" mask did not look much like Mickey: if anything, it was more like Donald Duck.
3. Len Deighton, *Goodbye, Mickey Mouse,* Ballantine Books, New York, edn., 1983, pp.18 and 92.
4. "Mr. Mussolini takes his family to see every Mickey picture," "The Cartoon's Contribution to Children," *Overland Monthly,* October 1933.
5. According to the *New York Financial World,* October 1933.
6. Cecil Munsey, *Disneyana: Walt Disney Collectibles,* Hawthorn Books, Inc., New York, 1974, p.128.
7. Illustrated, *ibid,* p.130.
8. Clipping identified only as "Boston, Mass, November 1933" in Disney scrap book.
9. Bernard C. Shine, unpublished thesis on Mickey Mouse memorabilia.
10. Munsey, *op. cit.,* p.110.
11. *Boston Transcript,* December 21, 1933.
12. According to the Huntington (W.Va) *Herald Dispatch,* December 18, 1933.
13. Philip French, *The Movie Moguls,* Weidenfeld & Nicolson, London, 1969, p.76.
14. Quoted, *ibid,* p.75.
15. John Betjeman, *Evening Standard,* London, 1 June 1935.
16. I am greatly indebted to the article "Mickey Mouse Meets Konrad Lorenz," by Stephen Jay Gould, *Natural History,* May 1979, for the correlation of Lorenz's findings and Mickey's development.
17. Christopher Finch, *The Art of Walt Disney,* Abrams, New York, 1973, p.49.
18. Maurice Sendak, *TV Guide,* Los Angeles, Ca., 11 November 1978.
19. E. H. Gombrich, *The Story of Art,* Phaidon, London 1972 edn., p.34.
20. *Loc. cit.*
21. *Ibid,* p.35.
22. John Betjeman discussed these problems in the *Evening Standard,* London, on 19 December 1934 and 6 February 1935.
23. *Time,* 16 February 1931.
24. *Claes Oldenburg, Drawings and Prints,* ed. Gene Garo, Chelsea House Publishers, London and New York, 1969, p.66.
25. Illustrated *ibid,* p.135.
26. Quoted *ibid,* p.134.
27. Coosje van Bruggen *Claes Oldenburg: Mouse Museum/ Ray Gun Wing,* Museum Ludwig, Cologne, 1979, p.3.
28. *Ibid,* p.65.
29. *Loc. cit.*
30. *Ibid,* p.67.
31. *Ibid,* p.71.
32. Bernard C. Shine, unpublished thesis on Mickey Mouse memorabilia.
33. Quoted Todd A. Brewster, "Happy Birthday, Dear Mickey Mouse," *Americana,* November/December 1978.
34. *Loc. cit.*
35. Bernard C. Shine, unpublished thesis on Mickey Mouse memorabilia.
36. Reported *New York Mirror,* 12 November 1933.
37. See picture of this presentation in *New York Herald Tribune,* 3 December 1933.
38. *New York Post-Standard,* 5 August 1935.
39. *Ibid.*
40. See *New York Post,* 11 June 1935.
41. Reported, *New York Journal,* 9 August 1935.
42. John Culhane, "A Mouse for All Seasons," 11 November 1978, p.51.

TIN TOYS

After 1920, when much of the inspiration for new toys came from newspaper comic strips, magazine features and the movies, popular, animated cartoon characters like Mickey Mouse were natural subjects for reproduction.

The manufacturers of tin toys were among the first to respond to the demand for Mickey Mouse toys, lithographing the designs on to tin plate and then machine pressing them. Designers were dispatched to see the Disney films, and they returned with hurriedly made sketches for reference. This hasty research

resulted in rat-faced Mickeys with teeth and hands with five fingers instead of the original's four — but they are much prized by collectors today.

Germany had been exporting one-third of its production of tin toys to the United States since 1900, and it was a German company, Johann Distler of Nuremberg, that created a tin-plated, wind-up, walking Mickey Mouse in just the style described above (page 47). Distler's Mickey Mouse toys bear a globe trademark. Many toys produced by other large companies may also be identified by a trademark or company title. However, there were a number of smaller, family firms whose output is unidentifiable but that produced high-quality, very collectible toys.

One such novelty is the five-fingered Mickey Mouse slate dancer (page 37). Possibly also made by Distler, it is simply marked "Made in Germany" and bears a registration number. This important toy is an excellent example of how a mechanical action can successfully recreate the animation of the screen. Novelty toys of this type were also operated by clockwork, hand-crank, gravity or rubber-band power.

Before the German government took it over in 1933, Tipp & Co. created another notable toy, a magnificent motorcycle with five-fingered Mickey and Minnie Mouse figures as riders. The attention to detail on this toy is remarkable; it is accurate even down to the tin Dunlop tires (page 49).

Other noteworthy German mechanical tin toys are a Mickey hurdy-gurdy, a drummer and a sparkler.

The wind-up hurdy-gurdy features a toothy Mickey turning the crank while Minnie dances to the tune on top. Mickey also appears to push the cart, but this is an illusion created by the cart's jigging in place as Mickey turns the crank (page 45).

The Mickey Mouse drummer (page 44) was produced in several variations. The flat, die-cut, lithographed Mickey figure, with a drumstick in each hand, has a simple lever, gear and spring mechanism. When the toy is operated, a lever inside the snare drum pushes the top of the drum upwards, to strike the drumsticks in quick syncopation.

The sparkler simply consists of a flat, die-cut, lithographed Mickey Mouse head on a sparkler mechanism, which causes colorful sparks to radiate from his eyes and mouth.

Trains were among the most popular tin toys. Nevertheless, one leading manufacturer of toy trains, the Lionel Corporation of New York, was in dire financial straits in the Depression and went into receivership on 7 May 1934. Mickey Mouse played a key role in the company's recovery. In 1934, Kay Kamen, Disney representative for all merchandising deals, granted Lionel a license to produce "a toy propelled by either mechanical or electrical movement, with or without tracks." The toy Lionel introduced was inspired by the ubiquitous Mickey Mouse. It was a small, wind-up handcar, packaged with an eight-section circle of gauge O track for just one dollar. Two versions of the handcar were produced: one features Mickey and Minnie pumping away around the track, while the other, designed to appeal to Christmas 1935 shoppers, has Santa operating the handcar with a toy Mickey Mouse peeping out of the top of his sack (pages 34 and 35). Both versions were wildly successful. Lionel distributed 253,000 and had to turn down orders for 100,000 more because of lack of production time. The toys' popularity drew attention to Lionel's more profitable line of trains and the company's receivership was discharged.

Lionel's English competitor, Wells O'London, produced a smaller handcar carrying celluloid figures with tin arms. The lithographed tin sides feature Pluto and Horace Horsecollar (page 35).

In 1935–6, both companies produced a Mickey Mouse clockwork circus train. In Lionel's version (pages 30–3), Mickey stokes the engine with a continual up-and-down movement created by a protruding rod striking the ties in the track. The Wells O'London circus train (pages 38–43) has a unique mechanism that allows Mickey to rotate, giving the illusion that he is actually stoking the engine, and the train's streamliner *Silver Link* 2509 locomotive was more modern looking than Lionel's New York Central type engine. Both versions were made to a scale of 1:45 and ran on gauge O track.

In 1935, Lionel also produced a freight and passenger train with a Mickey Mouse stoker car, and in 1936 the company introduced its last Disney toy, a Donald Duck and Pluto handcar.

Many Disney toys were made for younger children, too. For example, the Fritz Bueschel Company of Hackettstown, New Jersey, produced beautiful tin spinning tops between 1933 and 1939. Made in various sizes, the tops are lithographed with the Disney characters playing musical instruments and whistle as they spin.

Germany, England and the United States were not the only countries to make early Mickey Mouse tin toys. The Spanish company Isla also produced Mickey Mouse mechanical toys. In an action-packed sparkler toy, Felix the Cat (Otto Messmer's cartoon character) and Mickey Mouse light big cigars with a candle, and the action of the sparkler is visible through the candle flame. Another tin toy made by Isla has Felix hidden away in a basket, with Mickey holding the lid firmly shut as the cat tries to pop up. Both toys depict Mickey with a very toothy grin (page 46).

The United States also exported tin toys to Europe in significant numbers in the 1920s and 1930s, with novelty toys and Lionel trains especially popular. However, after World War II, tin toys lost their commercial dominance to plastic toys.

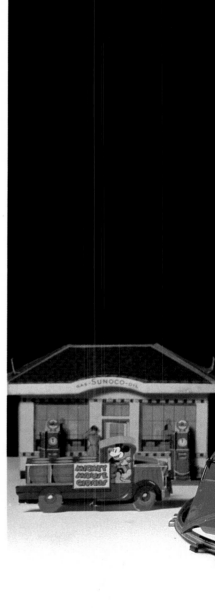

The circus train set is one of the most unusual – and also one of the most sought after – Mickey Mouse toys because of the strange combination of perishable and relatively durable materials used. Once assembled, the easily torn tent could be disassembled only with the greatest care. The engine, which weighs over 1lb (0.45kg), is in sharp contrast to the delicate and fragile paper tent. Rarely before or since can a toy have consisted of such diverse elements.

The illustrations on these and the following pages show the wealth of detail incorporated into this one toy by the manufacturers, the Lionel Corporation of New York, which, in the 1930s, had factories in Irvington, New Jersey. The tent itself is only 15in (38cm) high and 18in (46cm) wide. Most early Disney items were based on "swipe" art from the Disney Studio sheets. The circus tent is one of the few Mickey Mouse items (apart from books) for which entirely new art was created.

The engine (left) was Lionel's gauge O *Commodore Vanderbilt*, a streamliner used on many Lionel trains. The engine and tender are 7in (18cm) long, and, although the train itself is a wind-up model, there is a battery operated head-lamp. Included in the set were 84in (2m 13cm) of track, which had a trip mechanism on the centre tie, a feature supplied only with this particular Lionel train. The mechanism causes Mickey to shovel the imaginary coal as the train speeds around the oval track.

Accessories provided in the complete set included a 5in (13cm) high composition (compressed wood) figure of Mickey as a circus "barker," a miniature gas station and a cardboard cut-out of Mickey and Minnie.

The three Mickey Mouse circus cars (below), which completed the set, brought the overall length of the train to 30in (76cm). Colorfully lithographed, a combination of opaque and transparent inks allows areas of the tin to show through, creating a fascinating iridescent quality in many of the colors. The circus-animal car, dining car and band car are decorated with Horace Horsecollar, Clarabelle Cow, Pluto, two of the Three Little Pigs as well as Mickey and Minnie.

In 1935 a Sears-Roebuck catalogue advertised the complete set for sale by mail order for $1.79. The Mel Birnkrant Collection.

Perhaps even more famous than its circus train set is Lionel's Mickey Mouse handcar (opposite). First produced in May 1934 for that year's Christmas market, the handcar is credited with saving the Lionel Corporation from bankruptcy, for the company was in the hands of the receiver. Orders for 350,000 of the $1.00 handcars reversed Lionel's fortunes at a time when sales of its conventional trains were flagging. The body of the handcar is tin, and it is 8in (20cm) long and 6in (15cm) high. Designed to run on Lionel's gauge O track, the wind-up car is 2in (5cm) wide, and it was supplied with 72in (1m 82cm) of track. The composition figures have natural rubber tails and legs. Lionel made the handcar in four colors – red, green, maroon and orange – and the maroon version is the rarest. The Robert Lesser Collection.

Lionel's Santa handcar (left) is made of a combination of lithographed tin and composition. Produced in 1935, it was a seasonal toy, made in limited numbers. With Mickey Mouse peering out of the top of Santa's sack, the handcar ran on Lionel's gauge O track. It is 11in (28cm) long and 6½in (17cm) high, and came, complete with track, in a well illustrated box. The Robert Lesser Collection.

The English-made Mickey Mouse handcar (below) was produced in 1935 and 1936 by Wells O'London under its Brimtoy brand. The figures of Mickey and Minnie are of celluloid, while the body of the handcar is lithographed tin. The car is 7½in (19cm) long and 5in (13cm) high, and, as it moves along the track, a bell rings. The Robert Lesser Collection.

The rare paddle boat (below left) was produced in 1934. The wind-up motor moves the paddles back and forth to propel the boat, which is of lithographed tin and wood. The toy is 12in (30cm) long and 3½in (9cm) high. The box bears a Macy's label. The Robert Lesser Collection.

When the metal wire on the back of this lithographed tin Mickey Mouse is pressed, Mickey moves his legs and crashes the cymbals together, while his arms move, swinging the saxophone to one side to give the impression that he is playing. Made in Germany in the early 1930s, the toy is 6in (15cm) high. The Stefan R. Sztybel Collection.

Made in Germany, possibly by Johann Distler of Nuremberg, between c.1930 and 1931, the only known identification of the Mickey Mouse slate dancer (opposite) is the registration number 508041. The toy is lithographed tin, and it has a crank, wind-up mechanism. It is 6½in (17cm) high and 3½in (9cm) wide. The Robert Lesser Collection.

This Mickey Mouse circus train was made in England by Wells O'London, under its Brimtoy brand, between 1935 and 1936. The *Silver Link* engine, number 2509, features "Mickey the Stoker," who has a unique swivel action enabling him to shovel the coal efficiently. The three cars (below) – a circus-animal car, a band car and a dining car – were supplied with the engine, a circular track (not illustrated) and a tin circus tent (overleaf) in a cheerfully decorated box (far left).

The engine is 7½in (19cm) long and 2in (5cm) high, while the stoker's "tender" is 4in (10cm) long and 3½in (9cm) high; the circus cars are 6in (15cm) long and 3in (8cm) high. The train is 2in (5cm) wide, and it is made to run on gauge O track, measuring 1½in (4cm) between the rails.

Made to accompany the Wells/Brimtoy circus train
illustrated on pages 38–9, this tin circus tent is 5½in
(14cm) high and has a diameter of 8in (20cm). Illustrated
right and below are, respectively, the front and back of
the tent, while opposite is a detail of the entrance.

41

These illustrations from the Wells/Brimtoy circus tent (see previous pages) indicate the attention paid to detail by the manufacturers, as characters from the Disney pantheon circle the tent. The Robert Lesser Collection.

This Mickey Mouse drummer was manufactured by Nifty Toys and distributed by the George Borgfeldt Corporation in 1931. Made of lithographed tin, the toy bears the number 173 and is 7in (18cm) high. When a lever is depressed, the arms move up and down to beat the drum. The box has the "Luna" face trademark of Nifty Toys in each corner. The Robert Lesser Collection.

Made of flat, pressed tin, the Mickey the Musical Mouse toy (below) is 5½in (14cm) high and 9¾in (25cm) long. There were a number of variations on this toy, but the model illustrated is among the rarest. Probably manufactured by the Nuremberg company Johann Distler in the early 1930s, the words "Germany. By exclusive arrangement with the Ideal Films" appear on the base of the toy; the registered number is 508041. The three pivoted heads move when a handle at the back of the toy is turned to play a simple tune. The toy was distributed in the United States by the George Borgfeldt Corporation. The Stefan R. Sztybel Collection.

The Mickey Mouse hurdy-gurdy (right) is rarely seen in mint condition and complete with Minnie as seen here. Minnie is not attached to the toy – she simply lifts out, or, if the toy is inverted, falls out, and she is, therefore, easily lost. When Mickey cranks the handle, Minnie dances to a "rinky tink" tune. The lithographed tin toy is 8in (20cm) high and 7in (18cm) wide. Made in 1931, probably by Distler, it is marked "Made in Germany." The Mel Birnkrant Collection.

Mickey opening a basket containing Felix the Cat (below) was manufactured by the Spanish company Isla. The spring action of the toy raises the top of the basket and allows Felix to pop up. Made c. 1930, the toy is 5in (13cm) long, 4½in (11cm) high and 2in (5cm) wide. The Robert Lesser Collection.

Also manufactured by Isla, this rare sparkler (above) was not an authorized Disney toy. Mickey Mouse and Felix the Cat light their cigars on the sparks generated by the friction of flint on sandpaper, and the action may be seen through the candle's flame. Made c. 1930, this lithographed tin toy is 7in (18cm) high and 5in (13cm) wide; it is marked "LA 'ISLA' RS." The Robert Lesser Collection.

The five-fingered, walking wind-up toy (right) was manufactured by Distler c.1930–31. This early tin-plated toy has a natural rubber tail. The toy, which is 9in (23cm) high and 2in (5cm) wide, has the rat-like face and teeth that characterize early Mickeys. Only two examples of this toy are known to exist: the example shown here is complete, but unfortunately the other is in a state of disrepair. The Robert Lesser Collection.

This tin-plate and composition Minnie Mouse and pram (below) was made by Wells c.1933. The toy is 7½in (19cm) long, and a clockwork mechanism drives the two rear wheels. Photograph courtesy Sotheby's, London.

The motorcycle (right) was produced in Germany by Tipp & Co. for export to Britain in the early 1930s. The lithographed tin toy, which has a clockwork mechanism, is 10in (26cm) long, 6in (15cm) high and 2in (5cm) wide. The five-fingered characters are typical of the period. The Robert Lesser Collection.

CELLULOID TOYS

The introduction of celluloid revolutionized the toy industry, for celluloid, unlike tin, may be used to reproduce explicit detail in vibrant color. Although the manufacturers of tin toys had been the first to respond to the demand for Mickey Mouse toys, they were unable to compete with the quality and low production costs of celluloid.

Celluloid was originally used as a synthetic substitute for ivory. Its translucent quality combined with its infused color give celluloid a natural look. It also has the advantage of being decorative, relatively durable, lightweight and waterproof — excellent characteristics for water toys. However, the basic ingredient of celluloid, gun cotton, is highly flammable, and this factor eventually caused American manufacturers to impose a voluntary ban on the use of celluloid for toys.

Apart from being flammable, celluloid toys are featherweight and extremely delicate, and many have, inevitably, been damaged or broken. Even so, examples in good condition may still be found.

In the United States, celluloid production began in the 1860s, but by the end of the 19th century the technology moved to Europe. As early as 1901, German manufacturers were exporting celluloid toys to Gamage's of London. Throughout the *Belle Epoque*, up to 1914, such great department stores of Paris as *La Samaritaine* and *Aux Trois Quartiers* were selling a wide selection of celluloid toys and dolls. By the end of World War I, however, Japanese cottage industries were the leading producers and exporters of toys made of this material.

The rarest and earliest celluloid Disney character toys were those made in Germany from the early 1930s, and almost all were unauthorized. For example, the Rheinische Gummi und Celluloid Fabrik Company of Mannheim, Germany, produced a five-fingered Mickey, packed in a box imprinted with its tortoise trademark (page 57).

Throughout the 1930s, many celluloid Disney character toys were imported into the United States from Japan by such distributors as the George Borgfeldt Corporation of New York. Disney licensees in the United States included the Amloid Company, which specialized in celluloid rattles, and in Britain, Cascelloid Ltd produced Disney figurines, rattles, napkin rings and egg-timers. Some of the toys bore tissue paper labels imprinted "Mickey Mouse, copyright 1928 and 1930 by Walter E. Disney," but these dates refer to the Mickey Mouse copyright, not the date of the toys' manufacture.

Mechanical toys often combine celluloid and other materials such as wood and tin and have simple wind-up mechanisms. Figures that feature nodding heads use rubber-band power (page 53). Occasionally, celluloid Mickey images were added to other mechanical toys to increase their saleability (page 52). Although few wind-up toys were made during the 1930s, even the stationary celluloid figures give the illusion of animation. Functional household items such as pencil sharpeners, tape measures and place-card holders also came in the guise of celluloid Disney figures.

This pull-toy (top), with turning wheels, belongs to a group of simple children's toys, and, contrary to the belief of many collectors, it was licensed by Walt Disney. The colors are formed by separate pieces of tinted celluloid, which give the toy a brilliance not seen in the usual Disney celluloid figures, which are essentially moulded in white and painted. The image of Mickey is cleverly produced with the aid of wooden beads. This toy is 12in (30cm) long and 5in (13cm) high, and it was made, probably in Japan, in 1934. The Mel Birnkrant Collection.

The rubber-band wind-up mechanism and pendulum cause Mickey and Minnie to see-saw up and down. The two figures are celluloid, and the see-saw (teeter-totter) is tin. The toy is 4½in (11cm) high and 6in (15cm) long; it was made in Japan. The Bernard C. Shine Collection.

Mickey and Pluto (left) are made of celluloid and the cart is tin. The wind-up mechanism causes the cart to run along the floor and Pluto to bob up and down. Made in Japan c.1933, the cart is marked "© Walt Disney." The Mel Birnkrant Collection.

Mickey and Minnie (right) go motoring in a wind-up tin cart, which runs along the floor. Both Mickey and Minnie are made of celluloid, and overall the toy is 4in (10cm) high and 5½in (14cm) long. The Bernard C. Shine Collection.

Standing on a metal base, 3in (8cm) wide, the celluloid Mickey Mouse (far right) is 7in (18cm) tall. A rubber-band device causes Mickey to nod his head. Manufactured in Japan between 1935 and 1936, the figure was copyrighted by Walt Disney. The Robert Lesser Collection.

The cart (below right) has a wind-up mechanism and runs along the floor. Mickey and Pluto are both made of celluloid, and the cart is tin. The toy, which was made in Japan, is 3½in (9cm) high and 4½in (11cm) long. The "Coming Home" board game in the background was made by the Marks Brothers Company, Boston, Massachusetts. The Bernard C. Shine Collection.

This celluloid Mickey and Minnie (far right) are both 5in (13cm) tall. Their movable heads and arms are attached to their bodies by elastic. They were made in Japan. The Bernard C. Shine Collection.

When the box (overleaf) is opened, the "Mickey-in-the-box" pops up. Mickey is made of celluloid, and the box is made of paper-covered wood. The box is 3in (8cm) square when closed; when Mickey has popped up, the overall height is 6in (15cm). The toy was made in Japan. The L. Trickett Collection.

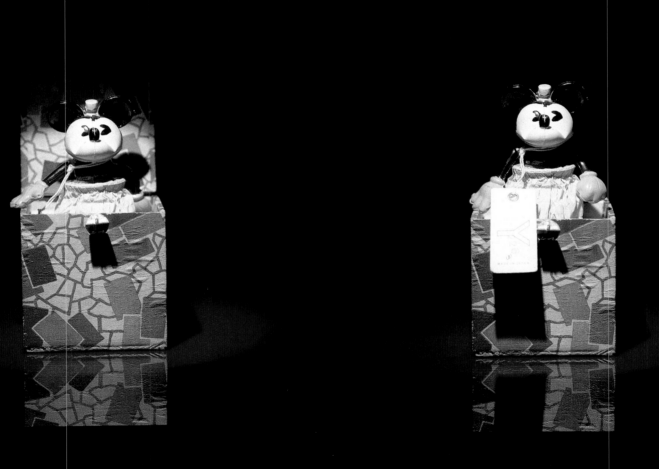

Made in Japan for the George Borgfeldt Corporation in 1934, the celluloid Rambling Mickey Mouse (right) is 7in (18cm) high, 5in (13cm) wide and 3in (8cm) deep. The figure has a steel tail for added balance. The Robert Lesser Collection.

When the wind-up mechanism is activated, Mickey and Minnie (below) twirl and turn to simulate dancing. This celluloid toy, which is 3½in (9cm) high, was manufactured in Japan. Variations include Minnie dancing with Elmer the Elephant and Donald Duck dancing with Elmer! The Bernard C. Shine Collection.

Mickey in a bathing suit and Mickey in a rubber ring (below centre and below right) were both made in Japan and are celluloid. Mickey in the rubber ring, which is both a toy and rattle, is 4½in (11cm) high; Mickey wearing a bathing suit is 5½in (14cm) high. The Bernard C. Shine Collection.

This rare five-fingered Mickey Mouse (opposite) is a celluloid vibrating toy; the ears are tin plate and the tail wire. The figure was manufactured in Germany by the Rheinische Gummi und Celluloid Fabrik Company, which was founded in 1873. The box bears the company's trademark, a tortoise in a diamond. Produced between 1929 and 1932, the toy is 6in (15cm) high, 4in (10cm) wide and 2in (5cm) deep. The Robert Lesser Collection.

Mickey Mouse

Nr. 7052

MADE IN GERMANY

When the wind-up mechanism is activated, the celluloid elephants (left and below) vibrate and shuffle about, bobbing their heads and flapping their ears. Distributed by the George Borgfeldt Corporation, the elephants were made in Japan c.1934, and they are 8in (20cm) high and 10in (26cm) long. Left: The Mel Birnkrant Collection; below: The Bernard C. Shine Collection.

This celluloid Mickey and his wooden rocking horse are 7½in (19cm) high. When the mechanism is wound up, the horse rocks while Mickey rides. The original cardboard box, which is also illustrated, is 8 × 7in (20 × 18cm). The Bernard C. Shine Collection.

TOYS OF OTHER MATERIALS

This lead figure of Mickey is 3¼in (8.5cm) high. It has the number 7506 stamped on one leg, and it was probably made in England. The same figure appears on other items such as metal ashtrays and match holders. Private Collection.

A cornucopia of Disney toys and games was produced under license between 1930 and 1938. Toy makers adapted many favorite old games to capitalize on the popularity of Mickey and Minnie Mouse, providing entertaining and educational pastimes for children of all ages.

One of the leading manufacturers of Mickey Mouse games was the Marks Brothers Company of Boston, Massachusetts, which produced board and skill games with bold, imaginative graphics in four colors. Among the company's wide range were a circus game, rollem, bean bag and scatter ball. One of the most popular was a target game, which consists of a free-standing tripod target of Mickey Mouse (the bull's eye is his stomach) and an enameled steel, spring-loaded gun, firing six rubber-tipped vacuum-cup darts (page 64).

A favorite with toddlers was the Marks Brothers Company's jack-in-the-box, with a pop-up head of Mickey in a box illustrated with a picture of Minnie Mouse. The cloth doll's head for this toy was made by the Knickerbocker Toy Company. Other items produced by the Marks Brothers Company were cardboard horns and noisemakers, jigsaw puzzles, kites, paint box sets, and sewing or yarn sets.

Many other toy makers also benefited from the sales appeal of Mickey Mouse appearing on their toys and games. Few items were designed for adults, but the Whitman Publishing Company of Racine, Wisconsin, designed playing cards for adults as well as for children (page 70). The decks were sold individually and in bridge sets with tallies and score pads. They were also available in both standard and miniature decks, the latter often featuring Pluto as the Joker. For children, Whitman created a special set of Mickey Mouse "Old Maid" cards, with Clarabelle Cow as the Old Maid.

The Marks Brothers Company, Hall Brothers and Chad Valley of Birmingham, England, all manufactured versions of "Pin the Tail on Mickey." The Marks Brothers Company's version came packaged in a colorful box showing a blind-folded Minnie eagerly approaching the target while Mickey blindfolds one of the Three Little Pigs. Both the Mickey target and the pin-on tails are made of durable linen and paper.

Chad Valley was a prolific producer of games, with titles and graphics on its products similar to those of the Marks Brothers but appealing more to an English market. Chad Valley's art tended to be subtler and the colors more muted than those used by the Marks Brothers. It produced Mickey Mouse snap cards, Mickey Mouse quoits (similar to horseshoes) and many other games for the European market as well as for home sales.

Mickey and his friends were featured on every imaginable type of toy — from Mickey Mouse safety blocks (building blocks with specially rounded corners) printed on alternate sides with letters of the alphabet or numerals and Mickey Mouse, to action toys with sound effects. One such popular toy was a Mickey Mouse telephone. There was also a wide range of Mickey push-and-pull toys many of which were made of wood and painted with non-toxic paints.

Disney's American distributor, the George Borgfeldt Corporation of New York produced what is reputed to be the first American-made, painted wood Mickey Mouse doll (page 75). Designed by Disney artist Burton "Bert" Gillett, it has movable arms, simple wooden hands — rather like lollipops — and a wire tail ending in a wooden ball. At the front of Mickey's red pants is a yellow panel bearing his name. In 1931, a more refined version with a painted composition head was produced. This was available with green, red or yellow pants and shoes and came in two sizes, 7¼ or 9¼ inches (18.5 or 23.5cm) high.

In the mid-1930s, Seiberling Latex Products Company, of Akron, Ohio, made Mickey Mouse dolls of hard rubber with movable heads (page 66). These little dolls, which were only 3½ or 6 inches (9 or 15cm) tall, were carefully painted and presented in colorful boxes decorated with Mickey and other Disney favorites. They are now increasingly rare because rubber can become misshapen when softened by heat, or it becomes overly hard with the passage of time. Seiberling also made inflated Disney dolls, including a four-fingered Mickey.

On a larger scale, wooden hobby-horses with Mickey Mouse heads, Mickey Mouse rockers, see-saws (teeter-totters) and even Mickey Mouse slides were produced. A vast majority of these toys and games have suffered the inevitable wear and tear of all children's toys and were eventually discarded, but collectors can still hope to make exciting discoveries.

This rubber Pluto (below) stands 4in (10cm) high and is 7¼in (18.5cm) long. He was made c.1934 by the Seiberling Latex Products Company, Akron, Ohio. Pluto is painted red, with black mouth, nose and ears, and with white eyes with black pupils. He is colored red because all Mickey and Pluto's early films were in black and white, and Pluto's later ochre color was not established until 1937–8, after which all shorts featuring Mickey and Pluto were made in color. The Ward Kimball Collection.

This display of early red and white Mickey images is composed of figures made between 1931 and 1934. In the centre is an exceedingly rare bank, made of cast iron and still with its original paint. The bank is French and is marked *Déposé* (patented). Such banks were widely used in France by secondary school students as aluminum casting projects. As a result, many aluminum copies, each slightly different in form and color, have turned up to confuse collectors. The bank is surrounded by a variety of dolls made of wood or composition. The two on the left and right of the centre are examples of what is reputed to be the first Mickey toy to be manufactured by the George Borgfeldt Corporation in 1930 (see page 75). The whole display measures 14 × 36in (36 × 92cm). The Mel Birnkrant Collection.

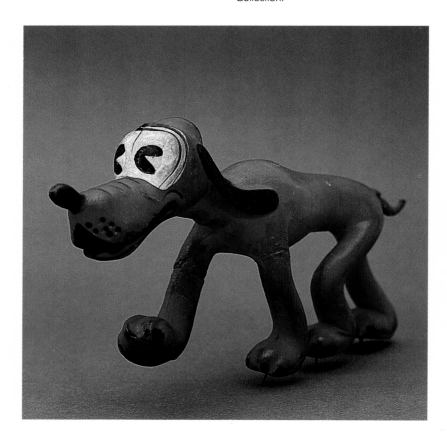

Manufactured by the Marks Brothers Company, Boston, Massachusetts, this cardboard target game (left) was made c.1934. The target itself has a diameter of 18in (46cm), and it came complete in a cardboard box with a three-legged stand, a metal gun and six suction darts. The Bernard C. Shine Collection.

This wonderful array of Mickey Mouse games were all made by the Marks Brothers Company. The display is 32in (81cm) high and 28in (71cm) wide. In the background are two versions of a bagatelle game, while in the centre is a Mickey Mouse hoop-la. To the side are scatter-ball games, which Sears-Roebuck sold for 21 cents each, promoting them as a means of helping children to "total figures." All these games were made c.1934. The Mickey and Minnie dolls hanging in front of the bagatelle boards are carnival figures with spring limbs, which were made in Japan. The Mel Birnkrant Collection.

The quoits game board (inset) was made by Chad Valley, Birmingham, England. It is 12 × 12in (30 × 30cm). Private Collection.

The painted wooden Mickey (left) can be manipulated into a variety of poses and is designed to stand on one foot or on one hand. Manufactured for, and distributed by, the George Borgfeldt Corporation, the toy is 4½in (11cm) high and is marked "Mickey Mouse © Walt E. Disney Pat. Dec. 16, 1930." The Stefan R. Sztybel Collection.

The Seiberling Latex Rubber Company, Akron, Ohio, produced a range of Disney figures including Mickey, Donald, Pluto, Elmer the Elephant, Snow White and the Seven Dwarfs, the Big Bad Wolf and the Three Little Pigs. This rubber Mickey (opposite below left) is 3½in (9cm) high; Seiberling also produced a 6in (15cm) version. The Bernard C. Shine Collection.

The moulded cheesecloth Halloween mask (opposite centre below) is part of a complete child-size Mickey costume. Made by the Wornova Manufacturing Company, New York, c.1934, the outfit came complete with a long, black rubber tail. Wornova also made costumes for such Disney characters as Minnie and Clarabelle Cow. The Bernard C. Shine Collection.

The French rubber Mickey (opposite below right) is 7½in (19cm) high. It is thought by some collectors to have been made as a toy for cats. The Bernard C. Shine Collection.

The Mengel Company, St Louis, Missouri, made this child-size rocking toy (above), which is 24in (61cm) high and 35in (90cm) long. The Mengel Co., which made several versions of the toy, was licensed between 1935 and 1939. The Bernard C. Shine Collection.

Distributed by the George Borgfeldt Corporation, this Mickey Mouse circus pull toy (left) was manufactured by Nifty. Mickey and Minnie are made of wood, with composition ears, and the tin box base has wooden wheels. As the toy is pulled along, an axle crank pumps the paper bellows under Minnie and makes a squeaking sound. The toy is 12in (30cm) long and 4½in (11cm) wide. The Ward Kimball Collection.

The Mickey Mouse circus game illustrated on these two pages was made *c.*1935 by the Marks Brothers Company, Boston, Massachusetts. It is 20in (51cm) high and 9in (23cm) wide. A marble is "thrown" down the line by the force of gravity from Mickey to Minne in order to ring a bell and score points. The lithographed illustrations on the cardboard box are intricate and colorful. Sears-Roebuck offered the game for sale at 89 cents in 1935, when four glass marbles were included in the box. The Bernard C. Shine Collection.

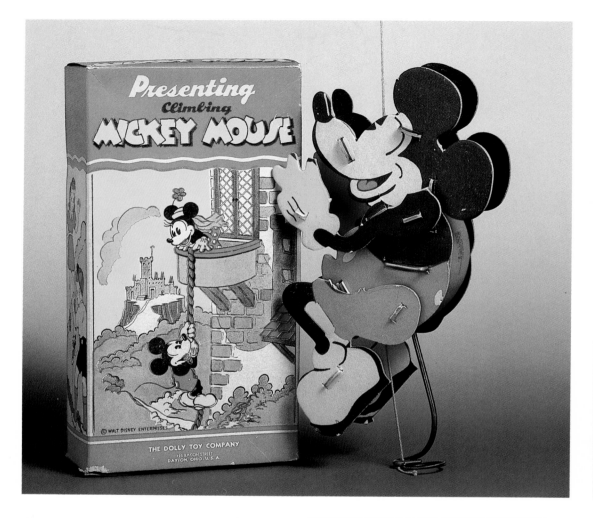

The "pin-the-tail-on-Mickey" (below) was made by Chad Valley, Birmingham, England. The box is 12 × 12in (30 × 30cm), and the tails are of paper. The L. Trickett Collection.

The climbing Mickey Mouse (above) is unusual in being a mechanical toy that is made entirely out of paper, cardboard and string – apart, of course, from the mechanism inside. When the string is pulled taut, Mickey climbs to the top. Mickey is 9in (23cm) tall and is marked "Pat. Applied for © Walt Disney Enterprises No. 74." The toy was made by the Dolly Toy Company, Dayton, Ohio, in the early 1930s. The Stefan R. Sztybel Collection.

The Whitman Publishing Company, Racine, Wisconsin, produced a range of Mickey Mouse playing cards. Illustrated right is a box of two packs of bridge cards, which came complete with score pads and tallies. The box measures 5 × 7in (13 × 18cm) and was made c.1935. Whitman's range included Mickey Old Maid cards, in which Clarabelle Cow was given the dubious distinction of being Old Maid, as well as cards featuring Minnie. The Bernard C. Shine Collection.

The play piano (right) was manufactured by the Marks Brothers Company, Boston, Massachusetts, in 1935. A combination of wood, glass and cardboard, the piano is 10in (26cm) high, 9in (23cm) wide and 5in (13cm) deep. As each key is depressed, the cardboard cut-out figures of Mickey and Minnie perform an animated dance. Behind Mickey and Minnie, Horace Horsecollar, Clarabelle Cow, Pluto and the Fiddler Pig are lithographed on to the wooden framework of the piano. Other versions had the Big Bad Wolf and all three of the Little Pigs in the background. In 1935 Sears-Roebuck offered the play piano for sale at $1.00. The Robert Lesser Collection.

The Fun-e-Flex Mickey, Minnie and Pluto (bottom illustration) have the same painted composition heads, wood-jointed bodies and movable limbs as those shown on the sledge. Mickey and Minnie are 7in (18cm) high; Pluto is 6in (15cm) long. Although Mickey and Minnie were manufactured in this form from 1931, Pluto was not made until 1934. As well as red, the figures were available in yellow and dark green. The Mickey and Minnie figures with four-fingered hands were also produced by Flex-e-Toys for the George Borgfeldt Corporation. Both are 7in (18cm) high, and they are standing in front of a 1931 Studio model sheet used by animators to help them draw the characters. Minnie's hat and flower are not original. The Bernard C. Shine Collection.

Made of wood, paper and metal, the "Choo Choo" (right) has a crank on the back axles that activates the bell-striking mechanism. The toy, which is 8½in (22cm) long and 3½in (9cm) wide, is marked "Choo Choo No. 432 © 1938 Walt Disney Enterprises." The Ward Kimball Collection.

The N.N. Hill Brass Company, East Hampton, Connecticut, made this pull toy (below) *c.*1935 for Walt Disney Enterprises. N.N. Hill was licensed between 1933 and 1942. String through the hole in Mickey's fist is used to pull the toy along, and, as Mickey is pulled forward, a metal "bead" in the bell tinkles as the wheels tumble forward. The toy is 13in (33cm) long, 7in (18cm) high and 4in (10cm) wide. Other versions featured Donald Duck and Pluto. The Ward Kimball Collection.

This larger version of the Fun-e-Flex Mickey Mouse (see also pages 72–3) is 9¼in (23.5cm) high. The cloth-covered wire tail has a wooden knob on the end, and the body is jointed and fully flexible. The figure is marked "Mickey Mouse Des. Pat. 82802 by Walt Disney" and was available in red and yellow as well as green. Made in the early 1930s, the toy was distributed by the George Borgfeldt Corporation. The Stefan R. Sztybel Collection.

Thought to be the very first American-made Mickey Mouse toy, Mickey (below) is made of wood, leatherette and rope. The hands, arms and legs are jointed, and when Mickey's tail is pushed down, his head bobs up. Designed by Disney artist Burton "Bert" Gillett (see page 10), the toy was manufactured by the George Borgfeldt Corporation in 1930. The figure is 6¼in (16cm) high and is marked "C. 1928–1930 by Walter E. Disney Des. Pat. APd for." The Stefan R. Sztybel Collection.

The Mickey Mouse Globe Trotters promotion, organized by Kay Kamen in 1937, was one of the most popular brand promotions. Participating bakeries gave away an envelope containing a colourful map measuring 20 × 26in (51 × 66cm), such as the N.B.C. (National Biscuit Company) one shown here. Children followed a race around the world between Mickey and the Big Bad Wolf. Twenty-four picture cards to be pasted on to the map came with the bread, and Mickey Mouse Globe Trotters membership badges, such as the two illustrated on page 114, were provided with the map. Private Collection.

The jig-saw puzzle (below) measures 9½ × 14in (24 × 36cm); it was made by Chad Valley, Birmingham, England. Private Collection.

The delightful Christmas jig-saw puzzle (right) was made by Vera Puzzles, Paris, France. It measures 7 × 8¾in (18 × 22.5cm). The Bernard C. Shine Collection.

Imp. de Vaug_ard, Paris.

77

DOLLS and PUPPETS

The first soft Mickey Mouse doll was designed by 14-year-old artist, Bob Clampett, from sketches he made during a Disney cartoon showing at the Fox Alexander Theater in Glendale, California. He had been commissioned by his aunt, Charlotte Clark, a shrewd woman who appreciated the marketing potential of such a doll. In January 1930 she and young Clampett took the 12in (30cm) high prototype to the Disney Studio, seeking permission to go into production.

The Disney brothers, Walt and Roy, were charmed by the doll. Charlotte began a limited production, which the Disneys purchased for distribution to friends, business associates and visitors to the Studio. When a photograph of Walt Disney with one of the Mickey Mouse dolls appeared in *Screen Play Secrets* and other periodicals, public interest was aroused and demand for the dolls was overwhelming. By November 1930, Charlotte

and her helpers were producing up to 400 dolls a week, but even this number was not sufficient to meet all the orders.

The Mickey Mouse dolls came in several sizes, were made of velvet with felt ears and were stuffed with kapok (a fine, cotton-like material). The distinguishing features were the single-line smile and eyes set parallel to the body (page 80). These Mickeys also had long, thin tails. Sometimes the words "Walt Disney's Mickey Mouse" were printed on the feet. In 1930, writing to the American toy distributor, George Borgfeldt, Roy Disney described the Charlotte Clark doll as "the truest character doll of its kind," and he quoted the enthusiastic response of buyers for various department stores.

In Britain, in October 1933 Dean's Rag Book Company, Rye, Sussex, began to produce Mickey and Minnie Mouse dolls by arrangement with Disney's London representative, William Banks Levy. These dolls, available in eight sizes, were made of velvet, with flat felt ears and hands. But the dolls had rather thin bodies, five-fingered hands and a toothy sneer, and neither Walt nor Roy was happy with them. Efforts were made to improve the dolls, and later versions had more rounded bodies and no longer had teeth. Nevertheless the Disney brothers were still dissatisfied, and they eventually banned their import.

In 1931 the George Borgfeldt Corporation began producing soft Mickey Mouse dolls made of velvet in six sizes, ranging from 6 to 18 inches (15 to 46cm) high. These dolls were unacceptable to the Disney brothers, however, as they did not hold their shape well compared with the Charlotte Clark dolls. Ironically, the Clark doll could be distributed only through Borgfeldt, because of the company's contract with the Disneys. Borgfeldt also distributed the doll manufactured by Dean's Rag Book Company until their importation was banned.

After several months of trying to get Borgfeldt to improve the quality of *his* doll, the Disneys released Charlotte Clark's patterns to the public through the McCall Company of New York City. McCall pattern No. 91 contained patterns for Mickey and Minnie Mouse dolls in three sizes, with instructions in English, French and Spanish. It was released early in 1932 and continued to sell until 1939.

Another manufacturer whose products pleased the Disney brothers was Margarete Steiff & Company of Germany (page

88). The company's beautifully made Mickey Mouse dolls came in six sizes. The smallest size is made of felt, the others of velvet, with mother-of-pearl buttons on their clothes. The Minnie Mouse dolls are also beautifully dressed and equally colorful. Both Mickey and Minnie have facial features similar to those of the Charlotte Clark dolls, but they carry the Steiff trademark: a metal tag punched through the left ear, with an orange label attached. They also have a round paper label stitched to their chests, bearing the name of the character and followed by "Copyright Walt Disney." In addition, on many of the dolls the sole of Mickey's shoe is marked "Steiff dolls."

From 1934, the Knickerbocker Toy Company of New York City also produced dolls that were satisfactory to the Disney brothers. The earliest standard versions were in velvet or duvetyne, and they were advertised as being in "cuddle or stand-up models."

In 1935, the company dressed Mickey in various costumes. In one outfit he wears cowboy chaps, a sombrero and neckerchief and carries a lariat and pistols. In another he is dressed as a clown. Each Knickerbocker doll has a small, die-cut string tag, which reads "Mickey Mouse [Minnie Mouse] Licensed by Walt Disney Enterprises for the exclusive manufacture by the Knickerbocker Toy Co. Inc., New York." Charlotte Clark designed a number of dolls for this company, including ones of Donald Duck, Pluto and Goofy. Many of these bear "Charlotte Clark Creation" labels.

Among the many kinds of Mickey Mouse playthings that were manufactured were hand puppets and glove toys. Margarete Steiff & Company and Dean's Rag Book Company created Mickey Mouse hand puppets or glove toys that were distributed in the United States through the George Borgfeldt Corporation.

Between 1933 and 1939 the Alexander Doll Company of New York produced marionettes of various Disney characters designed by Madame Alexander. All of these toys that could be manipulated added animation and a sense of reality to the characters. By far the most beautiful Disney marionettes are those made by the Hestwood Marionette Studio of Glendale, California (page 84). Marionettes of Mickey and Minnie Mouse were made exclusively for Bullock's department store, while several other Disney favorites, including Pluto and Donald Duck, were sold through such stores as Macy's. The Hestwoods were primarily puppeteers, and they performed with larger versions of the toy marionettes in their shows.

Charlotte Clark made the large Pluto (below) in the late 1930s. He is 16in (41cm) tall. The little Pluto is also illustrated on page 73. The Ward Kimball Collection.

Mickey and Minnie (right) were both made by Charlotte Clark. Mickey, who was made 1930–4, is 19in (48cm) high; Minnie, who was made rather later than Mickey, but before 1939, is 16in (41cm) high. The Ward Kimball Collection.

This collection of Mickey and Minnie dolls (opposite), all manufactured in the early 1930s, illustrates the diversity of dolls made. The Bernard C. Shine Collection.

This large, velour stuffed Mickey, with googly eyes is 16in (41cm) tall. He was probably made by Dean's Rag Book Company in the early 1930s. The L. Trickett Collection.

This Minnie (below) was made by Merrythought Toys, Ironbridge, Shropshire, England. In 1932 the company registered Movietoys as a trademark, and it specialized in a wide range of soft toys, including Mickey. Both the Mickey and Minnie produced by Merrythought had unusually long string tails. This Minnie is 12in (30cm) tall. Private Collection.

Established in 1903 to make rag books for children, Dean's Rag Book Company, Rye, England, produced velvet and velour plush Mickey and Minnie dolls in several sizes. Illustrated right are a 12in (30cm) tall Minnie and an 18in (46cm) tall Mickey. The dolls were made with "Everipoze" jointing, so that the limbs could be bent in any direction. Mickey's eyes are movable discs, and Minnie's are fixed and button like; the other facial features are printed. The Robert Lesser Collection.

These Mickey and Minnie marionettes are from a series that included Horace Horsecollar, Clarabelle Cow, Donald Duck, Pluto and the Three Little Pigs. They were made by the Hestwood Marionette Studio, Glendale, California. Mickey and Minnie were made exclusively for Bullock's department store, and on the right soles of the Mickey and Minnie illustrated here (left) are printed paper stick-on labels reading "Manufactured for Bullock's Wilshire by licence arrangement with Walter E. Disney, creator of Mickey Mouse." The other characters went to such prestigious stores "back East" as Macy's. Between 1933 and 1934 one thousand copies of each character were made. All the puppets illustrated here are 12in (30cm) tall, and they are made of composition, wood and cloth. In the late 1970s and 1980s, Bob Baker Marionettes recreated limited edition versions of some of the marionettes, which may be identified by a brass plaque on the handle and the words "©Walt Disney Productions" on the feet. Mickey and Minnie: The Ward Kimball Collection; Mickey: The Bernard C. Shine Collection.

Dean's Rag Book Company (see page 82) started to produce Mickey dolls in October 1933, eventually making them in eight sizes. They can be distinguished by their toothy sneer and rather rat-like faces, and a registration number may be found near their necks. Private Collection.

This group of five early — and unauthorized — Mickey Mouse dolls (left) was found as old stock in a toy shop in the north of England. Although rather primitive, each doll is slightly different and has individual facial features. Made in the early 1930s, they were probably produced by someone to earn a few pennies. Each doll is 18in (46cm) tall. Private Collection.

The Knickerbocker Toy Company, New York, manufactured Mickey and Minnie dolls designed by Charlotte Clark. Available in velvet and in three sizes, the dolls sometimes had composition or wooden shoes so that they could stand more easily. Private Collection.

Among the most desirable of all Mickey Mouse dolls are those made by Margarete Steiff & Company, Inc., Germany, which were imported to America by the George Borgfeldt Corporation. Steiff dolls may be identified by the small metal button trademark in the ear. Mickey Mouse dolls were made between 1931 and 1934, and they were modelled on sculptured clay figures. Made of velvet, the Mickey Mouse opposite is 7in (18cm) tall; other Steiff Mickey Mouse dolls were 5in (13cm) and 9in (23cm) tall. The buttons are genuine mother-of-pearl. This doll has a closed mouth, although some were produced with painted open mouths. The Robert Lesser Collection.

A rare and early Mickey (left), possibly German. Note the long whiskers and mother-of-pearl buttons. Private Collection.

This 7in (18cm) Steiff Mickey (below) is marked "Design Patent 82802." Made of velvet in 1931, there is a wire armature to keep the body upright. This Mickey is in excellent condition and has the ear tag and original label. The Stefan R. Sztybel Collection.

FIGURES

A variety of ornamental Mickey Mouse figures in porcelain, wood, glass and metal was produced during the vintage years. Most were made in Japan, but some were manufactured in Germany and in England. Many Mickey Mouse ornamental figures are made of bisque — a porcelain clay that has been fired once but not glazed. The figures were hand painted with a water-soluble paint. A few glazed ceramic figures were also made with the color fired into the clay.

The porcelain figures manufactured in Japan were usually unmarked though on occasion a paper label printed with the words "Mickey Mouse design patent 82802 by Walter E. Disney" was applied to the base. Other figures had mould numbers incised on the base. The quantity and variety of these bisque figures is a bit overwhelming. The Bisqueography on pages 174-6 is a relatively complete list of the Mickey, Minnie, Pluto, Goofy, Horace and Clarabelle bisque figurines manufactured in Japan in the vintage years.

Rosenthal China of Germany produced exquisite porcelain figures of Mickey and Minnie in black and white, the figures bearing Rosenthal's trademark of a single rose. However, this high-quality merchandise was produced only until 1935, and Rosenthal porcelain Mickeys are rare and greatly sought after.

Britain's output of ceramic Disney figurines was limited, but, unlike German companies, British pottery manufacturers continued production throughout the vintage period. One series of pieces 4in (10cm) high features single figures of Mickey, Minnie, Donald, the Three Little Pigs and other Disney characters on toothbrush holders. These are marked "Genuine Walt Disney Copyright — Foreign," and they were distributed by S. Maw & Son of London.

In total, nearly a hundred different bisque figures were produced by Japan, Germany and Britain between 1930 and 1938 before the outbreak of World War II put an end to their importation into the United States.

Though identical moulds were used for both glazed and bisque figures, the glazed ones are larger because of the difference in the degree of shrinkage. Ceramic clay shrinks between 3 and 5 percent, while porcelain clay shrinks as much as 15 or 17 percent. Glazing after the first firing slightly increases the size of the figures.

Examples of identical figures produced in both bisque and glazed clay include a toothbrush holder featuring Mickey and Minnie, side by side, and a Mickey figure washing Pluto's face.

Some Mickey and Minnie bisque figurines have tails that resemble black candle wicks. Some figures have movable arms. Many, but not all, pairs or sets of bisque figurines have a mould letter and number incised on them.

Usually, serial numbers with an identical prefix letter indicate a pair or set. For example, a matched pair of Mickey and Minnie figurines are numbered A116 and A117, and the figures in a set of Mickey playing baseball are numbered S64, S65 and S67. On the rare occasions when two different figurines bear the same number, it is probable that they came from different manufacturers. Another reliable guide to the completeness of a set is the accompanying box — if you are lucky enough to find figures with their box. Sets of figures often came in attractively decorated boxes, as in the case of four bisque figures of Mickey playing a quartet of musical instruments (page 94). This set was made in Japan and imported into the United States by George Borgfeldt.

Ornamental figures were produced in a variety of sizes, from 1¼ to 9 inches (3–23cm), and some were functional as well as decorative. For example, apart from toothbrush holders, there were ashtrays, match holders, egg timers, mustard jars, pencil holders and even scent bottles. These were distributed in the United States by the George Borgfeldt Corporation as early as 1932.

Clay was not the only material used for ornamental figures. Radiator caps or car mascots, designed in bronze and chrome finishes, were manufactured by the Desmo Corporation of Birmingham, England. The action-posed characters came individually or as a Mickey and Minnie Mouse couple (page 96). Other ornamental figures, made in Germany, included one very handsome series in cast metal, featuring Mickey in various poses. He is shown sitting in an overstuffed chair, holding an umbrella, holding a score tally and so on.

Other materials used for figurines included wood composition and even soap.

This Mickey and Minnie are carved wood, and they date from *c*.1933. In the early 1930s several carousels appeared in France, all made up entirely of Disney characters and all – apparently – carved by the same hand at the *atelier* of H. Devos, Angers.

The figures seen here stood atop one such carousel. The ears, which are completely round balls, are, in a way, more accurate representations of the film characters than the flat discs of the usual three-dimensional mouse, for in the films, of course, Mickey's ears are always seen as round no matter which way he turns his head. The eyes, which have led some collectors to speculate that the figures may be of a later date than 1933, appear to be modelled on the rolling disc eyes of the earliest Dean's Rag Book dolls. The flower is missing from Minnie's hat, and it is not known what the figures originally held: here Mickey holds a 1931 Borgfeldt parade cane that was used in a Mickey Mouse Club parade. Mickey is 39in (99cm) tall, and Minnie is 38in (96.5cm) tall. The Mel Birnkrant Collection.

Two Mickey Mouse perfume bottles, probably French and made in the early 1930s. The left-hand bottle is made of separate glass sections joined by metal springs. Mickey's head lifts off to allow access to the scent bottle's stopper. The J. Haley Collection.

The right-hand bottle is marked "3/66/83 *809" and is stamped "50." It is 4½in (11cm) high and 2¼in (5.5cm) wide. The body is glazed porcelain, the head is metal and the ears tin, and there is a rubber ball in the back of the head, which, when pressed, sprays perfume from Mickey's snout. The Stefan R. Sztybel Collection.

Mickey's head forms the lid of this ceramic pot, which was made in the early 1930s, possibly in Germany. The 6in (15cm) high pot is impressed with the word "Foreign," and the manufacturer's number "8264" is stamped on the neck. Private Collection.

The bisque figurines (above right), with the toothy rodent grins characteristic of early work, are 2in (5cm) high. They were made in Germany c.1931. The Mel Brinkrant Collection.

The perfume bottle (right) is similar to the right-hand bottle opposite except for the color of Mickey's pants. The Mel Birnkrant Collection.

The bisque figurines – Mickey Mouse Minstrels – were made in Japan in the 1930s and imported to the United States in their millions. Each figure is 5¼in (13.5cm) high, and the set of four hand-painted figures includes Mickey playing an acccordion, a French horn, a banjo and a drum. In the background is a Mickey Mouse Song Book, c.1933, by Irving Berlin, Inc. of New York. The Bernard C. Shine Collection.

This very rare metal doorstop (above and right) is 7in (18cm) tall and sculpturally unusual in several respects: the head is turned, but the ears remain in frontal view; the shoes are completely out of proportion; and the bent right knee and protruding chest add to the appeal. The Bernard C. Shine Collection.

During the 1930s Joseph Dixon Crucible Company, New Jersey, produced a variety of pencil boxes featuring Mickey Mouse. The pencil box (left) is papier mâché and is 8½in (22cm) long, 5in (13cm) wide and ¾in (2cm) deep. Clearly marked A Dixon Product and with the registration number 2770, the box contains four pencils in a paper wrapper, the pencils also manufactured by Dixon. The box itself was made 1934–5. The Robert Lesser Collection.

The toothbrush holder (left) is impressed on the base "Reg. No. 789573, Genuine Walt Disney Copyright, Foreign." Probably English, it is 4in (10cm) high and was distributed by S. Maw & Son of London for export to the United States. Private Collection.

This bisque figure (below) was made in Japan c.1935. It is 9in (23cm) tall, 4in (10cm) wide and 2¾in (7cm) deep. The front of the base bears the words "Mickey Mouse" and the back, "Walt E. Disney". The Robert Lesser Collection.

This paper over cardboard box measures 5½ × 3½ × 1½in (13 × 9 × 4cm); it contained three bisque figures of Mickey as a baseball player, each figure being 2⅜in (6cm) tall. The L. Trickett Collection.

The double-figure ornamental radiator cap or car mascot (below) was manufactured by Desmo Corporation of England. The chromium figures are painted, and they were made in 1934. Mickey is 6in (15cm) tall and 5in (13cm) wide, and Minnie is 5¼in (13.5cm) tall and 4in (10cm) wide. The single-figure radiator cap (right) was also produced by Desmo in 1934. It is 5in (13cm) tall, 3in (8cm) wide and 4in (10cm) deep. It is also painted chromium. The Robert Lesser Collection.

These cast metal figures (left), which are probably lead, were made in Germany in the early 1930s. The left-hand figure is 3½in (9cm) tall, 4in (10cm) wide and 2in (5cm) deep; the centre figure is 4in (10cm) tall, 2½in (6cm) wide and 3½in (9cm) deep; the right-hand figure is 5in (13cm) tall to the top of the umbrella, 2in (5cm) wide and 2in (5cm) deep. The Robert Lesser Collection.

The pair of porcelain match holders/strikers flanking a vase were all made by Crown Devon (S. Fielding & Co. Ltd) of Stoke-on-Trent, England. Produced with the consent of Walter E. Disney and Ideal Films, each figure is 6in (15cm) high. Private Collection.

TIMEPIECES

In 1932, a buyer for the Montgomery Ward Company suggested to Kay Kamen, who had been appointed Disney's merchandise representative on 1 July 1932, that a Mickey Mouse watch would have great sales appeal. Kamen agreed. He commissioned preliminary sketches and submitted them to the Ingersoll-Waterbury Company, whose experience of mass marketing pocket watches dated from 1892. A patent design was submitted to the United States patent office on 22 May 1933, and the first Mickey Mouse watches were produced shortly thereafter. The patent was granted on 5 February 1934.

Ingersoll-Waterbury was another major company that had been on the verge of bankruptcy when it signed a Disney license with Kay Kamen. And once again Mickey came to the rescue. In Macy's department store in New York City alone, over 11,000 Mickey Mouse watches were sold in a single day. Eight weeks into production, Ingersoll-Waterbury increased its work force from 300 to 3,000 to meet demand!

At first, Mickey Mouse pocket watches and wrist watches were produced. The pocket watch has an engraved Mickey image on the back of the case and on the fob. The watch face features the figure of Mickey, and the second-hand dial is imprinted with three more rotating Mickeys. Complete with its colorful gift box, the watch sold for $1.50.

In the mid-1930s Ingersoll-Waterbury produced a similar watch, this one designed to be worn on a lapel. It had a black case, a red cord to attach the watch to the lapel and a glass lapel button containing an image of Mickey Mouse. On the back of the watch case is a silk-screened Mickey Mouse design (page 100). It sold for $1.50.

Ingersoll-Waterbury's first pocket watch has a high bow and crown (the bow is the loop to which the leather strap is attached, and the crown is the part used to wind the watch). The bow and crown of later versions are more streamlined. These pocket and lapel watches were discontinued in 1938. There are counterfeits about, but none of these has the embossing or the decorated box that came with the original.

The wrist watch has a simple, round face featuring Mickey Mouse, his yellow-gloved hands pointing to the time. The watch band came in two styles: leather, with metal, die-cut Mickey Mouse figures attached to the band at either side of the face, or in silverplate with the Mickey Mouse image cast into the bracelet, its details filled in with black paint (page 100). The latter version is preferred by most collectors. On the dials of the earliest Mickey Mouse wrist watches are the words "Mickey Mouse Ingersoll." On subsequent versions, the phrase, "Made in U.S.A." was added. In 1933, the retail price was $3.75; by 1935 it had been reduced to $2.95.

To promote its watches, Ingersoll-Waterbury established a miniature factory at the 1933–4 Century of Progress Exposition in Chicago, Illinois. People attending the fair could place an order and actually see their watches being assembled.

In 1935, Ingersoll-Waterbury produced a de luxe Mickey Mouse wrist watch with a chrome-plated case (pages 100 and 103). The face was changed to a squared-off oval, and the inset circular second hand dial contains only one Mickey image. The watch has a leather band and it came in a box featuring Mickey in a top hat (page 103). Inside the box is Mickey tipping his hat.

Character watches were among the most successful Disney merchandise licensed, and in 1939, a Mickey Mouse watch was among the items sealed in the time capsule at the New York World's Fair. Between 1933 and 1939, Ingersoll-Waterbury sold $4,771,490.96 worth, paying a royalty to Disney of nearly $250,000. From June 1933 to June 1935, over two and a half million Mickey Mouse watches were sold. Production slowed down during World War II with the consequent shortage of raw materials, but it picked up again when the war was over. By 1948, five million watches had been produced. In 1957, watch production reached a staggering 25 million, and Walt Disney was presented with the 25-millionth watch, especially made in solid gold.

Other Disney character watches were produced too, but the Mickey Mouse watch was the outstanding seller. Thanks to the accuracy of its pin-lever movements, it was as popular with adults as children: it became "cheap chic."

Ingersoll-Waterbury also produced a wind-up clock in a green metal case. A paper band with Disney characters printed on it encircles it on three sides, and on the clock face Mickey's hands move to indicate the time while his head nods.

An Ingersoll-Waterbury 4½in (1cm) square electric clock also has images of Mickey and his friends on a paper strip applied to the case. Mickey's red-gloved hands point to the right time. Packaged in an attractive, stand-up display box featuring the Disney characters, and with a pop-up flap of Mickey holding a sign reading "Ingersoll Mickey Mouse Clock," the clock retailed at $1.50.

This first group of Mickey timepieces, all much sought after by collectors, did not include an alarm clock. This oversight was corrected in 1934, when Ingersoll-Waterbury produced a Mickey Mouse "Wagging Head," animated alarm clock. The clock has a 30-hour movement and a circular case, finished in red or green. There is a special movement for Mickey's animated head. The clock sold for $1.39, through the Sears, Roebuck catalogue, and retailed at $1.50.

Although most Mickey Mouse timepieces were produced in the United States, Ingersoll Ltd, London, Ingersoll-Waterbury's British division, manufactured two styles of pocket watch, a wrist watch and a square, wind-up clock. The graphics on these are distinctively British. The earliest pocket watch features Mickey in bulbous shorts, with thin, straight legs and small shoes. On later versions he is better proportioned.

The English wrist watch is a smaller version of the pocket watch, and it has a plain leather strap without metal Mickey Mouse designs. The dials of both the pocket and wrist watches are marked for the 24-hour clock.

Ingersoll Ltd made two styles of wind-up clock, both with similar graphics. The company also imported American-made Disney timepieces, including the electric clock and the wrist watches. The clock dials are marked "Made in U.S.A.," as are some of the wrist watches.

The record sales of all these various timepieces clearly demonstrate that, from their introduction until well after the inclusion of one in the New York World's Fair time capsule in 1939, Mickey Mouse timepieces were indisputably the favorite timekeepers of children — and quite a few adults — around the world.

The first Mickey Mouse watch to be manufactured is seen here (below) complete with the original point-of-sale display, which is extremely rare as the display material was not distributed to buyers of the watch and was usually thrown out by the store. The Ingersoll-Waterbury Clock Company, Waterbury, Connecticut, first made this enormously popular watch in 1933, and the watch retailed at $2.98, 11,000 being sold by Macy's on the first day. The watch face has a diameter of 1¼in (3cm). The Bernard C. Shine Collection.

The Ingersoll-Waterbury lapel watch (below right) has a black circular band around the 2in (5cm) diameter face. The lapel watch, which was first produced in the mid-1930's, when it sold for $1.50, has the image of Mickey silk screened on to the enamel back. Attached to the lapel by a red cord, it was held in place by a glass button with the image of Mickey on it. The Robert Lesser Collection.

This Ingersoll-Waterbury wrist watch (left) has a face with a diameter of 1¼in (3cm). It was first produced in 1933. The Robert Lesser Collection.

The Mickey Mouse de luxe wrist watch (below) is shown complete with its original display card. Ingersoll-Waterbury made this de luxe version in the late 1930s. The watch face is 1⅛in (2.75cm) long. The Bernard C. Shine Collection.

This pop-up display box was used with the Ingersoll-Waterbury Mickey Mouse electric clock. The metal case of the clock was spray-painted in green, and a paper band with Mickey, Minnie, Clarabelle Cow and friends was pasted around the sides. The clock is 4¼in (10.5cm) square, and it was produced in 1933. A wind-up version was manufactured at the same time. The Robert Lesser Collection.

Made for the English market c.1933, this Ingersoll pocket watch has a face with a diameter of 2in (5cm). Not only has Mickey five fingers on each hand, he is also seen, for the first time, with a pink face! The L. Trickett Collection.

In this display of timepieces are a Mickey lapel watch (see page 100), and (top row, right) a Mickey pocket watch of 1933. The left-hand watch of the lower row, featuring the Three Little Pigs and the Big Bad Wolf, was also made in 1933, while the Donald Duck watch dates from 1939. All the watches were made by Ingersoll-Waterbury, and all have a face diameter of approximately 2in (5cm). The Bernard C. Shine Collection.

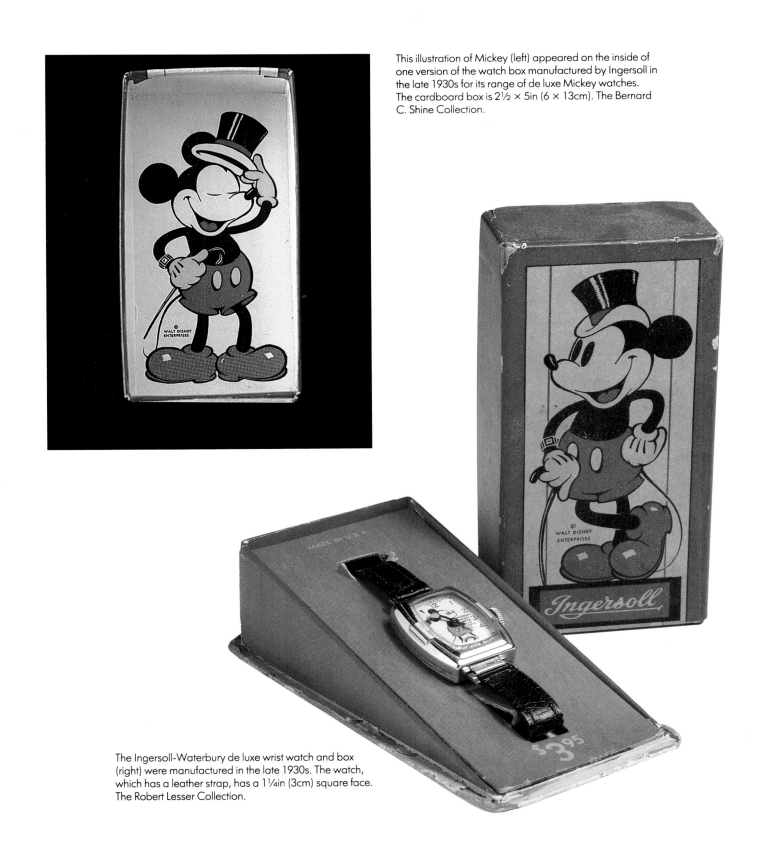

This illustration of Mickey (left) appeared on the inside of one version of the watch box manufactured by Ingersoll in the late 1930s for its range of de luxe Mickey watches. The cardboard box is 2½ × 5in (6 × 13cm). The Bernard C. Shine Collection.

The Ingersoll-Waterbury de luxe wrist watch and box (right) were manufactured in the late 1930s. The watch, which has a leather strap, has a 1¼in (3cm) square face. The Robert Lesser Collection.

TABLEWARE

Mickey and Minnie Mouse were the favored guests of children at both real and play dining tables during the 1930s. In addition to sets of well designed tableware consisting of plates, bowls, cups and glasses in china, beetleware (an early plastic), glass and metal, there was a good selection of tea sets in many of the same materials.

In the early 1930s, the Bavarian china imported by the Schumann China Company of New York included assorted tableware featuring Disney characters. This chinaware has a red and black Mickey Mouse trademark, with the inscription "Mickey Mouse—Trade Mark Registered" followed by "Authorized by Walter E. Disney — Made in Bavaria." The Mickey on the trademark appears to be walking and waving.

An American company that specialized in children's high quality chinaware was the Salem China Company of Salem, Ohio, whose tableware was marked "S.C. Co. Patriot China." To complement the chinaware, Libbey Glass Company produced "Safedge" glasses, featuring all the Disney characters in monochrome (page 110). These tumblers were widely used as promotional packaging for salad dressings and other food products.

The Paragon China Company of Staffordshire, England, produced Mickey Mouse tableware with captions accompanying the design. For example, an image of three staggering Mickeys, two of whom are smoking cigars, is captioned "Three Blind Mice." (The same designs appeared on postcards published by the Inter-Art Company of London, England.)

Besides children's tableware, many companies produced miniature tea sets of the kind illustrated opposite. Japanese companies introduced children's tea sets in lustreware with a high glaze. Usually, the china is tan or blue on a white base, and the pieces feature primitive-looking, hand-painted images of Mickey Mouse. The sets usually include cups, saucers, plates, a teapot, creamer, sugar bowl and serving tray. Not all of the pieces are marked, but some bear the imprinted words "Mickey Mouse copyrighted by Walt E. Disney. Made in Japan."

The leading name in the manufacture of children's lithographed tin tea-sets was the Ohio Art Company of Bryan, Ohio. The entire Disney family of characters is featured in four colors on the sets of dishes, cups and saucers, creamer, sugar bowl, teapot and serving tray, which have from 6 to as many as 23 pieces, packaged in attractive boxes. The Aluminum Specialty Company of Manitowoc, Wisconsin, also manufactured children's Mickey Mouse tea sets, and it produced coffee making sets with a percolator and baking sets, with egg beaters, measuring cups and baking pans.

Promotional pieces were also popular. For example, the Post Cereal Company of Battle Creek, Michigan, commissioned two major companies, William Rogers & Son and the Bryant Electric Company, to make such pieces. These were sold for 10 cents each, plus a Post Cereal box top. In this instance, they were not exclusively promotional pieces, for they could be purchased at retail stores, although at higher prices.

In 1937 William Rogers & Son, a division of the International Silver Company, Meriden, Connecticut, produced a silverplate teaspoon whose handle features Mickey with his hands on his hips and whose shank is inscribed "Mickey." This company also produced a variety of holloware and flatware pieces in sterling silver and silverplate, all featuring Mickey and his friends.

A best-selling item from the Hemco Molding Division of the Bryant Electric Company, Bridgeport, Connecticut, was a bowl with a stencil of a Disney character in the base, sometimes with the letters of the alphabet around the rim. It was produced in various colors, in the company's shatter-resistant plastic, which was called beetleware or safetyware. This excellent material for children's dishes is not flammable and is virtually unbreakable. It was also used for Mickey Mouse plates, mugs and tea party sets. The items were sold individually as well as in sets, in the full range of colors. As with so many other items of Disney merchandise, they were within the reach of all children — and, indeed, all children wanted them. Now, they are just as eagerly sought by collectors.

The miniature teapot and sugar bowl illustrated on page 104 are believed to be from the first Mickey Mouse tea set to be manufactured. They are china lustreware, and they were made in Japan and marketed by the George Borgfeldt Corporation in the United States. The teapot is 4½in (11cm) high, and the sugar bowl is 4in (10cm) high. This type of porcelain is known as lustreware because of the shiny, glazed finish, usually tan (a copper lustre) or, on white china, blue (a silver lustre). These sets featured primitive, hand-painted images of Mickey, Minnie, Donald Duck or the Three Little Pigs, and they normally included miniature cups, saucers, plates, creamers, sugar bowls, teapots and serving pieces. They were sold in boxes colorfully illustrated with pictures of Mickey and Minnie. Although not all the pieces were marked, the larger items were sometimes impressed with the words "Mickey Mouse Copr. by Walt E. Disney, Made in Japan." The Bernard C. Shine Collection.

The lithographed tin tea set of tray, teapot and six cups and saucers (left) was made c.1935 by Paton Calvert & Co. Ltd, England. The box is 12 × 9in (30 × 23cm). The Bernard C. Shine Collection.

The china bowl (opposite above), with Mickey and Pluto in the centre, has a diameter of 7½in (19cm). It was made in Bavaria, Germany, and imported into the United States by the Schumann China Company, New York, between 1932 and 1934. The china bowl (opposite below) is marked "© Mickey Mouse Walt. E. Disney." It has a diameter of 7in (18cm). The Bernard C. Shine Collection.

The two china plates illustrated overleaf were both made in Bavaria, Germany, and imported into the United States by the Schumann China Company of New York between 1932 and 1934. The Bavarian china included bowls, mugs, cups, saucers and plates adorned with pictures of Mickey, Minnie and the related characters, although no items feature Donald Duck as the line was manufactured before his creation in 1934. The Bavarian china is marked on the underside with a red and black, walking and waving Mickey, and it bears the words "Mickey Mouse – Trade Mark Registered," followed by "Authorized by Walter E. Disney – Made in Bavaria." Both these plates have a diameter of 7½in (19cm). The Bernard C. Shine Collection.

Libbey Glass-Owens-Illinois Glass Company of Toledo, Ohio, produced the glass tumblers with Mickey and Minnie on them in 1938. Libbey marketed a range of Disney character tumblers, which were widely used as promotional packaging for salad dressing, sandwich spreads and other food products. The glasses usually have a picture, in a single color, of Mickey, Minnie, Donald, Pluto, Clarabelle Cow, Goofy or Horace Horsecollar. Libbey called the range "Safedge" tumblers. The Minnie glass illustrated here is 5in (13cm) high; the Mickey glass is 4½in (11cm) high. Also illustrated (above left) is a store display for Libbey tumblers. The display is 12 × 9in (30 × 23cm). The Bernard C. Shine Collection.

The glazed earthenware bowl (above) is 3¾in (9.5cm) high and has a diameter of 8¼in (21cm). The bowl is marked "Czechoslovakia," and it was made in 1931. The Mel Birnkrant Collection.

These items from a tea set were made by Wade Heath &
Co. Ltd, Burslem, England. The cups have a maximum
diameter of 3½in (9cm) and are 2¾in (7cm) high. The
saucers are 5¾in (14.5cm) across. From c.1936 the
company's Disney items bore a circular mark with
the words: "Wadeheath Ware. Made in England".

BUTTONS and MISCELLANEOUS

Pin-back buttons have a long and prestigious history, but it was the simple design created by the Whitehead and Hoag Company of Newark, New Jersey at the beginning of the 20th century that made the buttons inexpensive and easy to produce for a mass market. Such buttons consist of a tin disc covered with a paper image, topped by a thin layer of transparent celluloid. All three layers are held together by a metal ring, which also holds a wire spring with which to attach the button to clothing.

The first Mickey Mouse celluloid pin-back buttons were issued in 1930 to members of the Mickey Mouse Clubs. The first Mickey Mouse Club was founded by Harry Woodin, under the direction of Roy Disney, at the Fox Dome Theater, Ocean Park, California. The original members' buttons bore an image of Mickey with outstretched arms and the words "Mickey Mouse Club." A separate design for the club officers, printed with the words "Chief Mickey Mouse," shows Mickey with his hands behind his back. By 1932 over one million children belonged to Mickey Mouse Clubs, and special buttons were issued for their birthdays.

Kay Kamen, Disney's astute merchandiser, introduced a line of Mickey Mouse pin-back buttons as promotional give-aways for retail stores and national advertisers. "Eat Sweeney's Butter Krust," invited Mickey on one button. Another publicized *The Sunday Herald and Examiner's* Mickey Mouse comics. Emerson Radio and Phonograph Corporation of New York issued one to advertise its famous, small-scale, four-tube Mickey Mouse radio for children. One of the most successful of Kamen's schemes was the Mickey Mouse Globe Trotters promotion. Participating bakeries gave away a map of the world and pin-back buttons of the kind illustrated on page 114 to children who followed a race around the world between Mickey and the Big Bad Wolf.

Bubble gum comic insert cards were introduced in 1933, when bubble gum manufacturers began packaging gum in flat, waxed paper wrappers. To prevent the gum from breaking, a picture card measuring 2½ x 3in (6 x 8cm) was included. Gum Inc. of Philadelphia, Pennsylvania, produced 96 different cards featuring Mickey Mouse. Each has a pun on one side and a riddle on the reverse, the answer to which appeared on the next card in the series. Two Mickey Mouse picture card albums were designed to hold the cards, and each album could be obtained

from local stores for five cents and five gum wrappers. Later, a further set of cards, numbers 97 to 120, featured Mickey with such popular film idols as Edward G. Robinson and Greta Garbo. These are now very rare, and no special album was produced for them.

Most desirable of all are the early 1930s Mickey Mouse bread cards. Each card features a recipe in which bread was the main ingredient, and bread manufacturers could have their name printed on the reverse of the card. There was also a free Mickey Mouse scrap book in which the cards could be mounted.

Mickey Mouse merchandise was primarily designed for children, but the products included many utilitarian items in addition to toys. Children could, and did, spend every waking moment with Mickey. Each day began with the r-r-ring of the famous Mickey Mouse alarm, a trip to the bathroom in Mickey Mouse pajamas, robe and slippers, then breakfast off Mickey Mouse tableware. When the children set out for school, they went armed with a Mickey composition tablet, readers, pencil box and other school accessories.

One of the leading manufacturers of school accessories was the Joseph Dixon Crucible Company of Jersey City, New Jersey. Dixon advertised cut-out boxes with pencils, ruler, eraser and pen, and compartmented boxes with as many as three drawers to hold pencils, crayons, pens, compass and assorted school supplies. The exteriors of Dixon's boxes are decorated with colorful Mickey Mouse graphics, and the interiors are lined with patterned paper, featuring various Disney characters.

At lunchtime, children opened up their tinplate Mickey Mouse lunch boxes, manufactured by the Geuder, Paeschke & Frey Company, Milwaukee, Wisconsin. The box has a lithographed four-color illustration of Mickey carrying *his* lunch box and books to school, while all his pals march around the base of the box. Specially designed handles secure the cover, which could also be used as a plate.

After school, children could be entertained by a Mickey Mouse gramophone, radio or projector, or could entertain themselves by playing a variety of scaled-down, Mickey Mouse musical instruments.

The 16-millimeter movie projector, made by the Keystone

Manufacturing Company of Boston, Massachussets, has a 50ft film capacity, with a rewind facility (page 114). It was made only in green, but has Mickey illustrations on all sides. Hollywood Film Enterprises released a selection of 8- and 16-millimeter home movies featuring Mickey Mouse and Donald Duck. The Movie Jecktor Company of New York City, New York, produced a de Luxe "Talkie Jecktor," which has a record player mounted on the projector. The Emerson Radio Company's small-scale, four-tube radio features Mickey Mouse in its decorations.

For the bookworm, there were Mickey Mouse lamps by which to read the enormous range of Mickey Mouse publications. The Soreng-Manegold Company of Chicago, Illinois, produced a Mickey Mouse armchair lamp that came with a parchment shade decorated with Mickey and Minnie Mouse motifs. Another of this company's lamps has a Mickey Mouse steel base and a choice of six Disney character shades (pages 128-9).

Other New York companies that manufactured children's table lamps and radio lamps were La Mode Studios and the Doris Lamp Shade Company. The well-designed, hand-painted sculptured bases feature various Disney characters, and the parchment shades have full-color reproductions of scenes from Walt Disney's motion pictures. Another New York manufacturer, the Micro-lite Company, made battery operated "Kiddy-Lites," which include a battery and standard bulb.

Children's outdoor play could include a digging session with a Mickey Mouse spade or sprinkling the flowers with a watering can. The versatile Ohio Art Company of Bryan, Ohio, made colorful sand pails, shovels, sand sifters and so on (page 122). And on rainy days, mother's little helpers could always turn their hands to making jello in a Mickey Mouse mould.

When bedtime arrived, a child probably brushed his hair with one of a range of Mickey Mouse brushes, washed with Mickey Mouse soap and, after cleaning his teeth with the aid of a Mickey Mouse toothbrush, put this away in a Mickey Mouse toothbrush holder.

The Lightfoot Schultz Company of New York made soap models of the Disney characters that sold throughout the United States. Having washed and brushed himself, the child snuggled down under a Mickey Mouse quilt, perhaps with a Mickey

Mouse hot-water bottle for extra warmth, with his head resting on a pillow covered by a Mickey Mouse case.

Indeed, such was Mickey's influence on children in the 1930s, that he was even used to promote savings in that money-conscious Depression era. The Automatic Recording Safe Company of Chicago, Illinois produced several Mickey Mouse banks (money boxes). One in the form of a savings suitcase has travel stickers reading "Mickey Mouse Thrift Hotel" and "Destination Wealth City." A second took the shape of a treasure chest. Both banks came individually packaged in colorful boxes. Collectors who find Mickey Mouse banks are fortunate; those who find them with their original boxes have even greater cause for self-congratulation.

The Glaser Crandell Company of Chicago used the idea of a Mickey savings bank to help sell its Mickey Mouse jam. When the jam had been eaten, a die-cut slot in the lid of the jar could be punched out to form a coin slot. The lid featured Mickey Mouse's face, and the slot was his mouth. The slogan "Feed Mickey for Wealth, Eat Jam for Health" is imprinted round the top edge of the lid. As a further incentive, for every two lids redeemed from subsequent jam purchases, the young Mickey Mouse "bankers" received a penny to boost their savings. Jars with the label still intact are rare and therefore very collectible, for the labels were usually removed when the jar became a bank.

Savings banks were manufactured in England and Germany for thrifty Disney fans overseas. One English version features a Post Office, while a German one is in the shape of a beehive and is decorated with Mickey and a swarm of busy bees. This latter model has a lockable money trap in the base (page 125).

One extremely rare French cast iron Mickey Mouse bank of the 1930s was made in two halves, which were then bolted together. The 9in (23cm) tall figure of Mickey has a coin slot in the top of his head. Subsequently, aluminum versions were made, probably from an original cast iron figure (page 123).

Thus, Mickey Mouse played a double role in helping to bring the Depression to an end. His Midas touch brought money pouring into the coffers of any manufacturer who featured him, and he also encouraged thrift in the children who would eventually help to restore their nation's prosperity.

Pin-back buttons featuring Mickey Mouse have been produced since 1930, when the first Mickey Mouse Club began; since then hundreds have been manufactured. Among those illustrated here are two Mickey Mouse Globe Trotters membership badges (see page 76) and (left, centre row) a give away from one of the original Mickey Mouse Clubs, in this instance, at the Fox Hollywood Theater. The Bernard C. Shine Collection.

The jewelry brooches (left) are wood composition and were made by the Brier Manufacturing Co., Providence, Rhode Island, which was licensed from 1935 to 1942. Each brooch is 1½in (4cm) high. The Bernard C. Shine Collection.

The three badges illustrated below are enamelled metal. The left-hand Mickey is 1¼in (3cm) high; Mickey in the centre is ¾in (2cm) high; and the right-hand Mickey is 1¼in (3cm) high. The L. Trickett Collection.

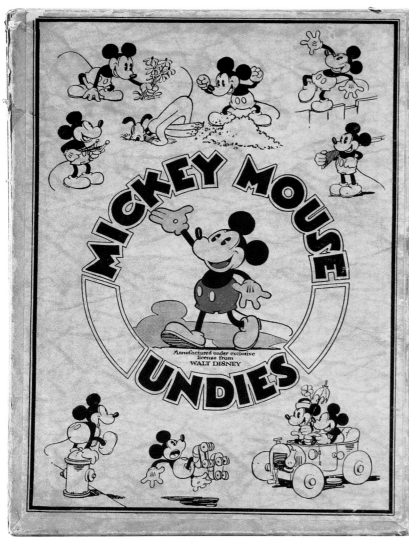

The Mickey Mouse undies box (left), which may have contained apparel made by the Norwich Knitting Company, Norwich, New York, is 11 × 9in (28 × 23cm). The Mickey and Minnie soap figures, both with their original boxes, are 5in (13cm) tall. They were made by D.H. & Co., London, England. The Bernard C. Shine Collection.

The hairbrush (below left), which is seen with its original box, has a celluloid and foil back and real bristles. It is 2in (5cm) at its widest point. The L. Trickett Collection.

The aluminum jelly mould was made by Sellman & Hill Ltd, England, in 1936. It is 3in (8cm) high. The Bernard C. Shine Collection.

This is a rare, painted version of the table radio made by the Emerson Radio & Phonograph Corporation, New York, which was licensed between 1933 and 1940. With it is the even rarer original box. The more usual version of this radio is made of pressed wood syroco and is dark brown. The radio is only 7in (18cm) square, yet it has sculpted relief images of Mickey on all four sides – playing a tuba, piano, bass fiddle and flute. The radio was provided with a heavy card, which was meant to get hot, and an exceedingly long aerial. The Mel Birnkrant Collection.

An early and rare album (below) of six 10in (26cm)
78 r.p.m. records, produced by His Master's Voice, a
division of The Gramophone Co. Ltd, England. The six
records are "Three Little Pigs," "Who Killed Cock
Robin?," "The Pied Piper," "The Band Concert," "The
Grasshopper and the Ants" and "Mickey's Moving Day
and Farmyard Symphony." Private Collection.

One of the rarest of all Mickey Mouse merchandise items
manufactured by the Emerson Radio & Phonograph
Corporation, New York, is the record player (right), which
was made for one year only – 1934. It is 21 × 13in
(53 × 33cm). The Mel Birnkrant Collection.

The home projector (opposite) is made of tin and is
10½in (27cm) high. It has a hand crank, and it was made
by the Keystone Manufacturing Co., Boston. Keystone
used an ordinary electric light bulb and hand crank to
project 16mm Mickey films. The Keystone projectors were
green, with attractive decals of Mickey applied to the
sides. The projectors came packaged in beautiful
four-colored boxes, which showed Mickey, Minnie and
Pluto watching Mickey cartoons on the screen. The
Keystone Film Catalogue that accompanied the projector
listed 48 Mickey film titles in 10-foot to 100-foot lengths.
Prices ranged from 35 cents to $3.50 a reel. The films
came in a variety of illustrated boxes. The Bernard C.
Shine Collection.

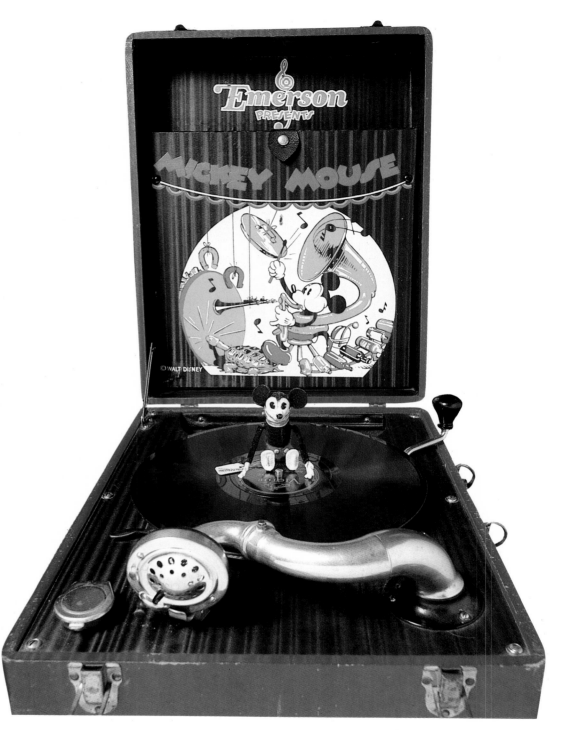

The George Borgfeldt Corporation distributed the tin drum (left), which was made in 1931. The drum is 18in (46cm) across and is marked "© W.E. Disney." The Mel Birnkrant Collection.

Edward Sharp & Sons Ltd, Kreemy Works, Maidstone, Kent, England, used this tin (opposite right) for its Mickey Mouse toffee between 1934 and 1935. The tin, which contained 4oz (113g) of toffee, is 6 × 7in (15 × 18cm) and 6¼in (16cm) high. The Robert Lesser Collection.

The banjo and saxophone (left) are 17in (43cm) and 15in (38cm) long respectively. The banjo was made by Noble & Cooley Co., Granville, Massachusetts, which was licensed between 1935 and 1939. The saxophone was made in Czechoslovakia and is marked "Czechoslovakia HARPO." It was marketed in the United States by the George Borgfeldt Corporation. The Bernard C. Shine Collection.

The drums and tambourines (above) were made by Noble & Cooley Co. The larger drum has a diameter of 10in (26cm) and the smaller one is 6½in (17cm) across. The tambourine has a diameter of 9in (23cm). The Bernard C. Shine Collection.

The Mickey Mouse bubble gum wrapper of waxed paper, which is 2½ × 3¼in (6 × 8.5cm), was made by Gum Inc. of Philadelphia, which was licensed between 1933 and 1937. As well as Mickey Mouse gum, a card came with the wrapper, and a Mickey Mouse picture card album could be obtained for five wrappers and a nickel. Two card albums, each containing 48 cards, were produced, but, although a third series of 48 cards featuring Mickey with various movie stars was printed, no special album was provided for the series. The Bernard C. Shine Collection.

The Mickey Mouse scissors (below right), 3in (8cm) long, were made in 1937. The Bernard C. Shine Collection.

Although looking more like Donald, this gas mask (below), issued to children in England during World War II, was known as the Mickey Mouse gas mask. Seen here with its original box, which is 6in (15cm) high and 4½in (11cm) wide, the gas mask has written on it "lot 22. Sep 1939. 8HCR," and on the blue band at the front, "G.C. Mk.III" and, at the back, "M.B.39." Inside the mask is written "AVON 11–39 36D." Private Collection.

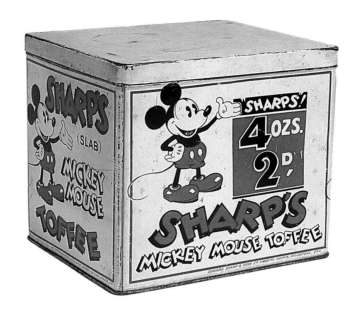

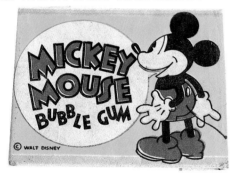

The leading name in lithographed tin Disney toys during the 1930s was the Ohio Art Company, Bryan, Ohio. The company featured Disney characters on a wide variety of toys, including tea sets, laundry sets, washing machines, carpet sweepers, sand sets, shovels, pails, watering cans and drums. The quality of the art and four-color reproduction was excellent. Ohio Art Co. was licensed between 1933 and 1942, and during the late 1930s many of its items were dated. The merchandise featured entire scenes with Mickey, Minnie, Donald, Pluto, Horace Horsecollar, Clarabelle Cow and other members of the gang. Some of the sets of items came in attractively illustrated boxes, a few featuring Disney characters, others just showing children at play.

Illustrated here (left) are two of the range of tin buckets manufactured by Ohio Art. The top bucket is 5¼in (13.5cm) high and the lower one is 6in (15cm) high. The tin watering can was made *c.*1933; it is 8in (20cm) high. The tin blade of the Ohio Art shovel (below) is 10in (26cm) wide and 7in (18cm) high; the handle is wooden. The Bernard C. Shine Collection.

Illustrated opposite is one of the few known examples of the original cast iron bank (money box) with its original paint. Hundreds of aluminium copies have turned up over the years, each a little different (see page 62), and recently collectors have been repainting them to emulate the look of the original bank illustrated here. This bank is 9in (23cm), and it is marked *Déposé*; it was made in France in 1931. The Mel Birnkrant Collection.

Complete with its original key to open the hinged metal door on the base, this composition bank (money box) was made by the Crown Toy Manufacturing Company, Inc., New York, in 1938. The bank is marked "Walt Disney Crown Toy," and it is 6½in (17cm) high. On this particular model, the makers forgot to paint on Mickey's orange glove below his left arm! The Ward Kimball Collection.

The still bank (above right) bears the words: "Mickey Mouse Bank. © Walt Disney. Be thrifty – save your coins." Mickey and Minnie look out of separate teller windows above the words "Deposit your money in the Mickey Mouse bank," and on the brass end trim, above the slot for money, are the words "For coins & bills." There is a hinged metal door of the base of the bank with a keyhole. The bank is 4in (10cm) long and 2¼in (5.5cm) wide, and it was made by the Eli Zell Products Corporation, New York, which was licensed 1933–4. The Ward Kimball Collection.

The Mickey Mouse dime register bank (below right) opens automatically after $5.00 in dimes have been deposited. Manufactured in 1939, it is 2½in (6cm) square and ⅝in (1cm) deep. The Robert Lesser Collection.

This tin bank (left) features a key opening money trap on the base. Made in Germany by Elbezet Company in 1934, it is 3in (8cm) high and has a diameter of 2½in (6cm). The Robert Lesser Collection.

The Mickey Mouse treasure chest (right) was produced by the Automatic Recording Safe Co., Chicago, Illinois, in 1935. Marked "Copyright W.D.E. and A.C. Co. 10–AX," the treasure chest is 3¼in (8.5cm) long, 2⅝in (6cm) high and 2¼in (5.5cm) deep. Below the words "We'll do our best to fill this chest," the figures of Mickey and Minnie uncover hidden treasure on the "Isle of Thrift." The Robert Lesser Collection.

MICKEY MOUSE TREASURE CHEST

BANK

This rare mechanical bank was made in England during the early 1930s. The early graphics – Mickey's rat-like teeth and five-fingered hands – suggest a date of between 1930 and 1932. The platform base is 3½ × 2in (9 × 5cm), and the bank is 7in (18cm) high and 3in (8cm) wide. On the side are the words: "By exclusive arrangement with The Ideal Films Limited. All rights reserved. Registered Number 508047." When Mickey's ear is pressed, his tongue comes out to receive your money! The John Haley Collection.

This plaster lamp (right) with paper parchment shade is in mint condition. Manufactured by the Soreng-Manegold Company, Chicago, in 1936, the lamp retailed at $2.95. The shade shown here is still in its original cellophane wrapping. It is rare to find this Mickey lamp with its original shade. Soreng-Manegold also made a figural lamp with Donald Duck standing at a post. The Bernard C. Shine Collection.

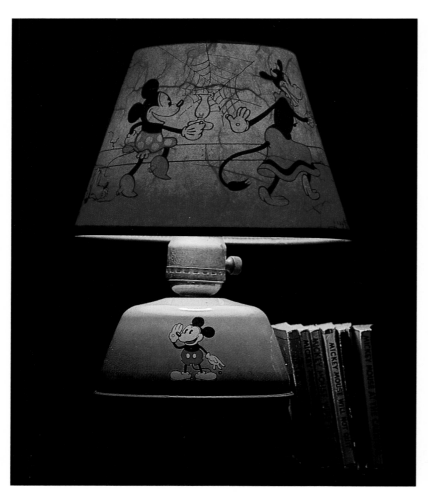

The Soreng-Manegold Company, Chicago, made this tin lamp with a paper parchment shade in 1935. It is rare to find such a lamp with its original shade as here. The base was finished in either green or ivory colored enamel, and there were six different shades available. The lamp is 11in (28cm) high, and it originally retailed at $1.00. Soreng-Manegold also manufactured Mickey Mouse sewing kits (retailing at 50 cents) and yarn holders (retailing at 25 cents) similar to the base of the lamp. The Bernard C. Shine Collection.

The Mickey Mouse light bulb filament, which is 5in (13cm) high, was manufactured in 1935. The Mel Birnkrant Collection; photograph by Jim Munsie.

PUBLICATIONS

From the beginning of the 1930s, the enormous interest in Mickey Mouse inspired great activity in the publishing world, and, in a very short time, there were books for children of every age. Mickey was helping children to learn the alphabet, and multiplication tables, teaching them how to tell the time and even appearing in a set of school readers, quite apart from his role as the hero in all kinds of adventure stories.

The very first publication was copyrighted "Walter E. Disney." Thereafter the books were copyrighted "Walt Disney Enterprises" and "Walt Disney Productions, Ltd," until December 1938, when the copyright changed again, to "Walt Disney Productions."

All of these books had tremendous visual impact and excitement, being illustrated throughout with the work of Walt Disney's Studio artists. Whether reproduced in black and white or full color, the outstanding graphics were a hallmark of the many publications featuring Mickey and the other Disney characters. Because of the high quality of the illustrations surviving publications from this golden era have soared in value in recent years.

The first Mickey Mouse book was published by Bibo and Lang of New York, in 1930, and it was illustrated by the Disney Studio. Entitled *Mickey Mouse Book*, its 16 pages contained a story, illustrations, a game and cut-out game pieces, a march and a song, all printed in black and green on cream paper stock. The story and game were originated by Bobette Bibo, the 11-year-old daughter of one of the publishers (page 146).

There were four separate printings, and although the editions were not individually numbered, the first printing may be easily distinguished. Page 8 of the first edition simply showed a picture of Mickey, centered on the page. In subsequent printings, however, the picture was lowered and a Mickey Mouse comic strip was positioned above it. After the initial printing, the back cover also featured a comic strip. The Mickey Mouse song, too, was changed. In the first edition it began "Fun--ny lit--tle ears ..." but in subsequent printings the new song began, "You're a hit what a hit. ..."

About 100,000 copies of *Mickey Mouse Book* were printed and sold in 5- and 10-cent stores or were given away with each purchase of the first Charlotte Clark Mickey Mouse doll.

In 1931, a second publication, *The Adventures of Mickey Mouse* Book 1, was published in full color by the David McKay Co. of Philadelphia, with a first printing of 50,000 copies. Available in both hard and soft covers, it attained first place on the children's best seller list and was in print until World War II (page 140).

Encouraged by the success of its first Mickey publication, McKay in the same year introduced a Mickey Mouse series, the first of which contained black-and-white comic strips reprinted from newspapers. A second title, also in black and white, was published in 1932; a third, in color, appeared in 1933, and a fourth, again in black and white, in 1934 (page 145).

By 1931, McKay had introduced flip-page story books. The *Mickey Mouse Movie Stories* contained stories illustrated with frames from Mickey Mouse films. In the bottom outside corner of each page were little line figures of Mickey (on right-hand pages) and Minnie (on left-hand pages) which, when the pages are flipped rapidly, produce the illusion of an animated cartoon with dancing figures. The book, which contains 11 stories, sold for $1.00.

Other publishers took up the novelty theme. Blue Ribbon Books, Inc., New York, produced a series of pop up books, including *The Pop-up Mickey Mouse*, which has three full-color pop-ups. Another Blue Ribbon book, *Mickey Mouse Waddle Book*, has characters that could be punched out of the pages, assembled and made to "waddle" down a ramp.

The Whitman Publishing Company of Racine, Wisconsin, also published an extensive list of story, coloring and painting books featuring Mickey and his friends. One of the most successful Whitman series was the Big Little Books. These measure only about 4in (10cm) square, but they contain between 300 and 400 pages and are lavishly illustrated. They sold for just 10 cents. Kay Kamen sold a few of the Big Little Books as promotional items: *Mickey Mouse Sails for Treasure Island* promoted Kolynos Dental Cream and *Mickey Mouse the Mail Pilot* was given away by the American Oil Company and by Procter & Gamble. In the late 1930s, a new series of books was issued entitled Better Little Books.

Walt Disney and the *Mickey Mouse Waddle Book,* "the story book with characters that come out and walk," now one of the most collectible of all Mickey Mouse publications.

Whitman made a feature of special sizes for its books. For example, it published the Wee Little Books, measuring a mere 3½ x 3in (9 x 8cm). Set number 512, copyrighted 1934, which contains six Mickey Mouse titles, was issued in a small cardboard box. A complete set of all titles and their box is now a rare and costly collector's item. The Whitman Big Big Book measures 7½ x 9½in (19 x 24cm) and is entitled *Story of Mickey Mouse.* It has 317 pages and is illustrated in black and white.

In Britain, Dean & Sons of London Ltd was the first publisher to release Disney books. In 1931 three titles appeared, two originated by David McKay, but the third was Dean's own *Mickey Mouse Annual.* This title was so successful that it became a yearly publication, continuing even through World War II. Another British publisher, William Collins, not only published many Disney books itself but also exchanged titles with American publishers like McKay and Whitman.

The first *Mickey Mouse Magazine,* containing stories, puzzles, jokes and illustrations, was started in January 1933 by Kay Kamen. It was given free to department store shoppers and movie patrons, and the series lasted for just nine issues, the final one appearing in September 1933.

Hal Horne, an advertising director and gag man for United Artists, edited another *Mickey Mouse Magazine* from November 1933. It was similar in format, size and style to the original, but was distributed by dairies throughout the United States to promote milk. Twenty-four issues were published, the final one appearing in October 1935.

Hal Horne published the third *Mickey Mouse Magazine* as a licensee of Kay Kamen (pages 134–5). This series was sold at news-stands throughout the United States, and the first issue was produced in May 1935 and priced at 25 cents. The initial print run was 300,000, of which only 150,000 were sold, and subsequently the magazine's size and price were reduced. After the first nine issues, Horne relinquished his publishing rights to Kay Kamen who continued to publish the *Mickey Mouse Magazine* until 1940, when it was merged into a comic book.

The first Italian Mickey Mouse magazine, *Topolino,* was launched in December 1932. Hachette in France followed with *Le Journal de Mickey* in October 1934. Both magazines were published as large-format tabloids with a comic page for the cover. Both are still being published.

Disney's first London merchandise representative was William Banks Levy, who, in 1936, produced *Mickey Mouse Weekly* (pages 136–7). The initial print run of 400,000 was increased to 450,000 for the second issue, and eventually reached over 600,000 copies a week. A number of smaller publications were printed during the vintage years, including the *Official Bulletin of the Mickey Mouse Club* which began in spring 1930 and was issued twice a month thereafter until December 1932.

Since that first Mickey Mouse book came out in 1930, Disney publications have appeared in no fewer than 46 countries, in 36 languages. Consequently, in the area of publications there is great scope for collectors, and even though much early material was printed on poor quality paper that quickly deteriorated, a great deal still remains.

One of the rarest and most eagerly sought after of all the Mickey Mouse books, the *Mickey Mouse Waddle Book* is shown here fully assembled. The book contained a story and cut-out walking models of Mickey, Minnie, Pluto and Mickey's horse Tanglefoot. When the book is opened (opposite above), the cut-out figures are revealed. Once punched out, however, the characters almost immediately fall apart when handled. Copies with the figures not punched out are rare; rarer still are those with the figures punched out and still intact. This display measures 11 × 30in (28 × 76cm) and shows the figures "waddling" down the ramp.

The book was published by Blue Ribbon Books Inc., New York, in 1934. There were 33 pages, and the book came with a decorative paper band, which held an envelope containing the ramp and brass hinges needed to assemble the full display. The book sold for $1.00. The Mel Birnkrant Collection.

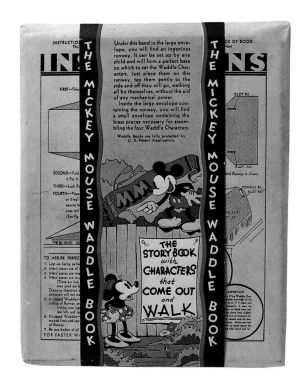

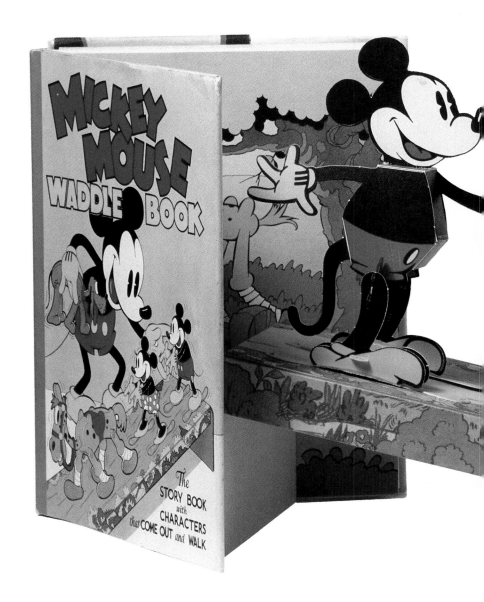

The third *Mickey Mouse Magazine*, published by Hal Horne from 1935, was the first series to be sold at news-stands and through subscriptions: earlier magazines were purely give-aways, distributed through movie theaters and, later, dairy companies. The slogan used to launch the magazine, with the June-August edition (opposite), was: "A fun book for boys and girls to read to grown-ups." Walt Disney was so pleased with the magazine that he ordered six subscriptions for the Orthopaedic Hospital School in Los Angeles (one of his favorite charities), and when Mary Pickford saw the magazine, she liked it so much that she arranged for Hal Horne to buy unsold copies, which she then distributed to hospitals.

Mickey as Santa adorned the cover of volume 3, number 3, in December 1937,

while Mickey and Minnie appeared on the front of volume 1, number 9, in June 1936. Donald and Mickey playing football were seen on volume 2, number 2, in November 1936, and Mickey, Minnie and Goofy squeezed into a car for the August 1937 edition, volume 2, number 11. The magazine measures 13½ × 10in (34 × 26cm) and has 42 pages.

Hal Horne found himself in severe financial difficulties and asked Kamen to buy him out. Kamen took over the magazine in June 1936 and continued to publish it until 1940. The magazine survived until volume 5, number 12, in September 1940, by which time demand had begun to fall and the magazine made way for a new publication, *Walt Disney's Comics and Stories*. The Walt Disney Archives.

Illustrated here are four covers from *Mickey Mouse Weekly*, a British publication first appearing in February 1936. *Mickey Mouse Weekly* was created by Walt Disney's official merchandise representative in Britain, William Banks Levy, and published by Levy in association with Odhams Press Ltd. It was such a successful venture that 450,000 copies of each issue were printed.

The cover of the edition for 25 April 1936, volume 1, number 12, featured, in addition to the familiar members of Mickey's gang, Max Hare and Toby Tortoise from the 1935 Silly Symphony *The Tortoise and the Hare*, while on the cover of volume 1, number 25, for 25 July 1936 are Madame Clara Cluck, Toby Tortoise and, in the foreground, the Practical Pig. In the month following this issue, the total circulation reached 600,000 copies a week. The Guy Fawkes issue, volume 2, number 92, for 6 November 1937, not only featured Toby Tortoise again but also included Abner Mouse from the 1936 Silly Symphony *Country Cousin*. Private Collection.

Mickey Mouse Bedtime Stories was published by The Sunshine Press, England, in 1935. Shown here are the front cover, the title page, the endpapers and one double-page spread. The book measures 9 × 7in (23 × 18cm), and it features Mickey, Minnie, Clarabelle Cow, Horace Horsecollar, the nephews and, making one of his earliest appearances in such a publication, Donald. Private Collection.

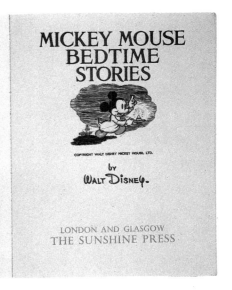

The twins went off to sleep dreaming of how Strongheart rescued the captive Princess.

MICKEY MOUSE BEDTIME STORIES

COPYRIGHT WALT DISNEY MICKEY MOUSE, LTD.

by
WALT DISNEY

LONDON AND GLASGOW
THE SUNSHINE PRESS

lonely and unhappy duchess who lived in a great big house standing in the midst of acres and acres of park land."

"What did the duchess look like, Auntie Minnie?" put in the excited children. "Was she as pretty as Uncle Mickey's princess or was she ugly and old?"

Minnie giggled and blushed as she caught Mickey's eye. "You mustn't interrupt, children," said the latter, "but if you must know I expect the duchess was very much like your Auntie Minnie." And the tale-teller went redder than ever in the face and giggled so much that Donald got quite annoyed.

"Quack! QUACK!" he cried.

54

"I expect the duchess was very much like your Auntie Minnie."

55

The Story of Mickey Mouse and the Smugglers was published by the Whitman Publishing Co., Racine, in 1935; it has 316 pages. Illustrated here is the revised edition, with new cover art, which is Big Big Book number 4062. The Walt Disney Archives.

The Adventures of Mickey Mouse Book 1 was published by the David McKay Company, Philadelphia, in 1931. It has 32 pages, and Book 2 appeared in 1932. This story book introduces readers to Mickey: "This story is about Mickey Mouse, who lives in a cosy nest under the floor of the old barn. And it is about his friend Minnie Mouse whose home nest is safely hidden, soft and warm, somewhere in the chicken house." Among Mickey's friends to be mentioned in the story are Henry Horse (later Horace Horsecollar), Carolyn Cow (later Clarabelle Cow) and Donald Duck, three years before his film debut in The Wise Little Hen (1934). This book was reissued – with a new cover – by David McKay to mark Mickey's fiftieth birthday in 1978. The Walt Disney Archives.

The David McKay Company, Philadelphia, also published *Mickey Mouse and his Horse Tanglefoot*. Appearing in 1936, the book has 60 pages and recounts how Mickey trades his old horse Tanglefoot for a truck. When the truck breaks down, Mickey buys back Tanglefoot, and they have a series of misadventures, working for the Ice Company, Katz Grocery Co., a dairy and a parcel delivery service, before defeating a gang of bomb-planting revolutionaries and becoming heroes. The Walt Disney Archives.

A Handful of Fun is a very unusual die-cut book of 12 pages filled with games and puzzles. It measures 5in (13cm) by 8in (20cm), and it was a give-away booklet, made by the Eisendrath Glove Company, Chicago, which, between 1933 and 1936 was a licensee for Mickey Mouse gloves and mittens. The Bernard C. Shine Collection.

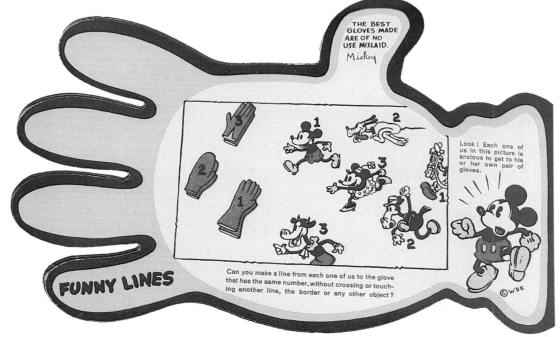

David R. Smith, Archivist of the Walt Disney Company, seen (right) holding a copy of *The Pop-up Mickey Mouse*. Blue Ribbon Books, Inc., New York, published this illustrated story with three pop-up pictures in 1933. It was one of a series of pop-up books, which included *The Pop-up Minnie Mouse, The Pop-up Silly Symphonies* and *Mickey Mouse in King Arthur's Court* (page 144). Stockists were told: "Display these books in your windows and you will supply a public demand that knows no season." The Walt Disney Archives.

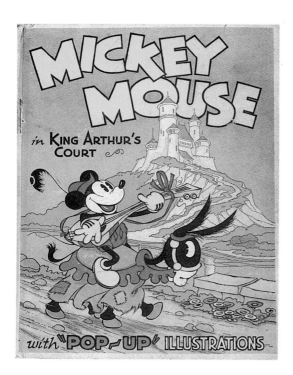

Mickey Mouse in King Arthur's Court, published by Blue Ribbon Books, Inc., New York, in 1933, was inspired by the Mickey Mouse short *Ye Olden Days* (1933). The book has 48 pages and four pop-up illustrations; it measures 10 × 7¼in (26 × 18.5cm). It was followed in 1934 by *The Pop-up Mickey Mouse in Ye Olden Days*, which used the same jacket illustration as the earlier book. The Walt Disney Archives.

Mickey Mouse Stories, published by the David McKay Company, Philadelphia, in 1934, has 62 pages. It was published in both hard and soft covers, and it was the follow-up to *Mickey Mouse Story Book*, which was published by McKay in 1931. *Mickey Mouse Stories* contains illustrations and text from *Pioneer Days*, *The Moose Hunt*, *The Castaway* and *The Delivery Boy*. The Walt Disney Archives.

In 1931 the David McKay Co., Philadelphia, published the first in a series of four books containing reprints of Mickey Mouse newspaper comic strips. The first, titled *Mickey Mouse Series No. 1*, is shown below, and right is the cover of the fourth in the series. Both volumes have 48 pages. The Bernard C. Shine Collection.

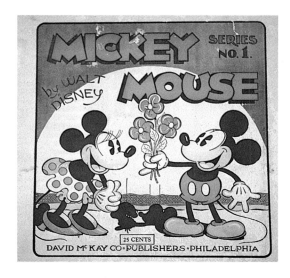

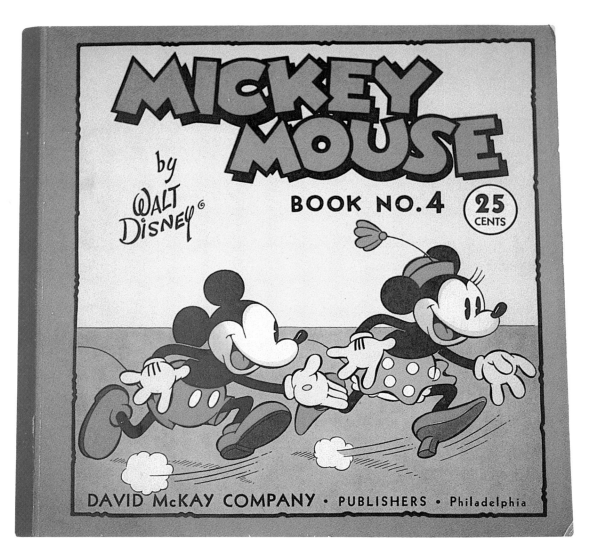

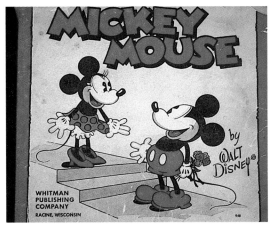

In 1933 the Whitman Publishing Co., Racine, published the 30-page *Mickey Mouse* (above), which measures 8½ × 10in (22 × 26cm). The cover illustration is the same as *Mickey Mouse Book No.3*, published by McKay in 1933. The Bernard C. Shine Collection.

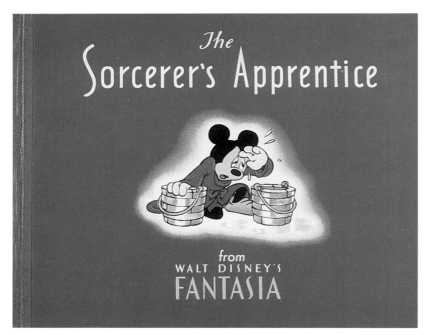

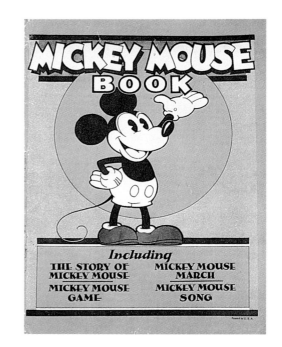

Published by Grosset and Dunlap, New York, in 1940, *The Sorcerer's Apprentice from Walt Disney's "Fantasia"* is one of a series of illustrated story books based on sequences from the 1940 animated feature *Fantasia*. This title is one of the scarcest in the series, the other title being published by different publishing houses. Other titles were *Ave Maria* (Random House, New York), *Dance of the Hours* and *Pastoral* (Harper & Brothers, New York), *The Nutcracker Suite* (Little, Brown, Boston) and a compilation volume, *Stories from Walt Disney's "Fantasia"* (Random House, New York). The Walt Disney Archives.

Mickey Mouse Book was the first story book featuring Mickey Mouse to be published. Sub-titled "Hello, Everybody," the book has 15 pages, and it was published by Bibo and Lang, New York, in 1930. The book originally included a Mickey Mouse game, a song and a march. The story and the game were by 11-year-old Bobette Bibo, daughter of one of the co-publishers. The story tells how Mouse Number 13 was thrown out of Mouse Fairyland because he was "always playing tricks and cutting capers." Landing on a roof in Hollywood, Mouse Number 13 meets Walt Disney, to whom he recounts his story. Mr Disney listens and then says: "You give me an idea for a series of comedies. I have an idea that I can make you a picture star.... But firs of all, we shall have to get you another name..." The book was originally sold by Charlotte Clark, who made the first Mickey Mouse stuffed dolls. Because this two-color book, printed in black and green, had only a short print run, copies are extremely scarce and come high on the list of items sought by collectors. The Walt Disney Archives.

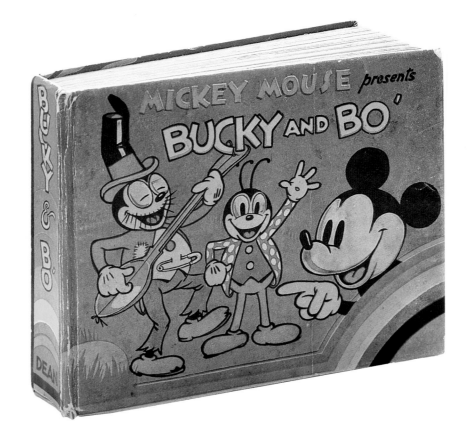

Dean & Sons Ltd, London, published *Mickey Mouse presents Bucky and Bo* (opposite below) *c.*1933. It was written by Earl Duvall and illustrated by Al Taliaferro, and the story featured Bucky Bug and Old Man Bo, who had appeared in 1933 *Silly Symphonies* and Sunday comic strips.

The book has 160 pages and measures 4½ × 5¾in (11 × 14.5cm). Private Collection.

William Banks Levy, Disney's merchandise representative in Britain, made a deal with Dean & Sons Ltd, London, to publish an original *Mickey Mouse Annual*. A new annual appeared each year thereafter, including throughout World War II. After the war an advertisement by Deans for the annual said: "For many years, the *Mickey Mouse Annual* has been the leading children's annual. It continues to be an established favourite, as it contains stories, verses, games, jokes and puzzles about Mickey Mouse and his friends, illustrated throughout with amusing Disney drawings in full colour. Each issue is eagerly awaited and sells out as soon as shown." The annuals measure 8½ × 6in (22 × 15cm) and have approximately 128 pages. Left: Private Collection; above: The Bernard C. Shine Collection.

The Mickey Mouse Sunday comic strip began in July 1932 and still runs today. Reproduced below is the strip for Sunday, 2 January 1938; it was written by Merrill de Maris, pencilled by Floyd Gottfredson and inked by Ted Thwaites. The Walt Disney Archives.

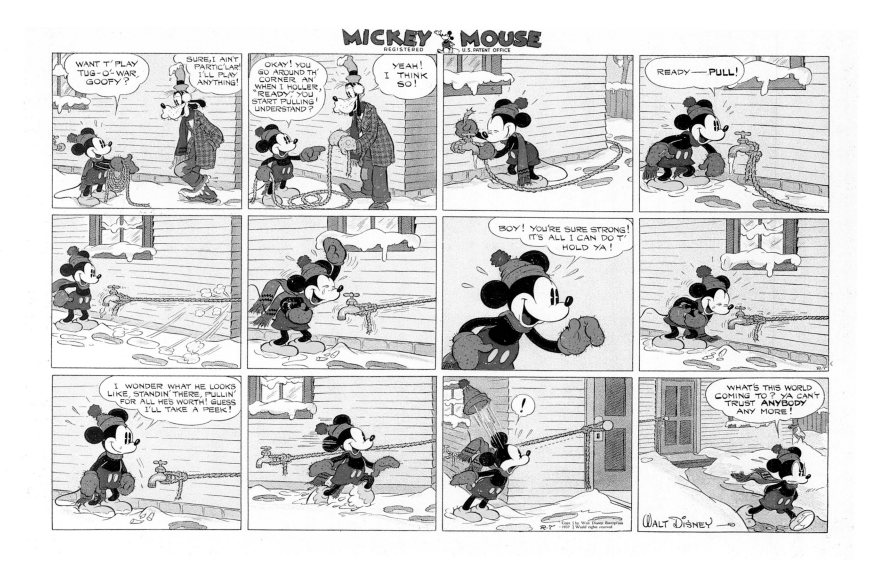

The strip for Sunday, 31 July 1938 was written by Merrill de Maris, pencilled by Manuel Gonzales and inked by Ted Thwaites and Bill Wright. The Walt Disney Archives.

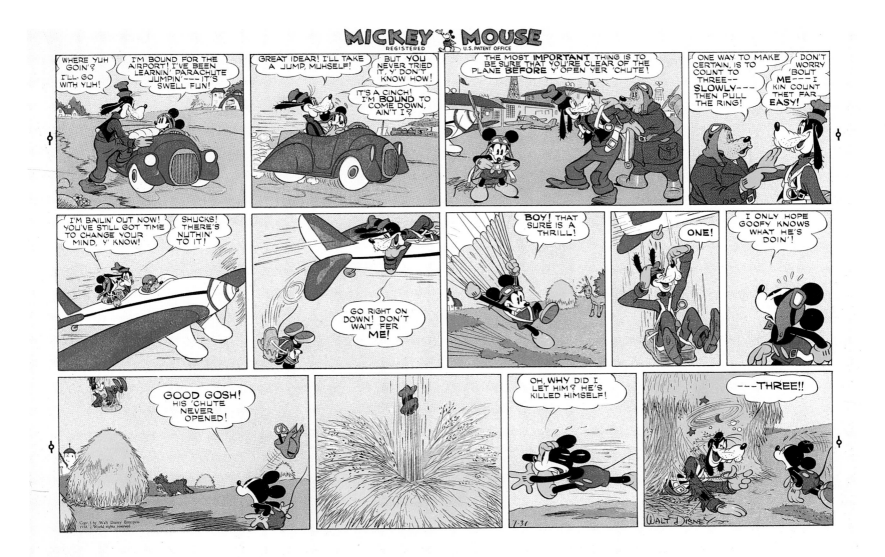

CARDS AND POSTERS

Shortly after the first Mickey Mouse cartoons were released in 1928, publishers in Holland, France, Italy, Belgium, Spain and Germany issued Mickey Mouse postcards. Many had dual-language captions, the second language being an English translation.

Publishers used names that were already well known to support this new character. For example, the French company Silvetas Artisticas, in its series number six, featured Betty Boop dreaming about Mickey Mouse (page 156), and the Inter-Art Company of London, England, used Charlie Chaplin and Douglas Fairbanks (page 157). Inter-Art produced the best quality Mickey postcards. Its cards have a white background that was created by overprinting a cream paper with white ink. Unfortunately, this made the cards very susceptible to surface damage. Moreover, the edges of cards tend to wear. Although the Inter-Art postcards presented an accurate physical reproduction of Mickey, they gave him personality traits not at all prescribed by Disney. They featured Mickey smoking big cigars, drinking and chasing women.

From 1932, the Walt Disney Studio sent out a specially designed card every Christmas to business associates and friends. The first featured a colorful illustration of Mickey, Minnie, Pluto, Horace and Clarabelle riding in a sleigh drawn by a reindeer. The printed verse reads "Walt Disney and Mickey Mouse Present Their Silly Symphony 'Season's Greetings'." The card folded to form its own mailer. In this way, Disney not only remembered his contacts and friends, but reminded them of yet another cartoon release.

The card sent in 1933 is a simple, one-sheet illustration of Mickey, Minnie and Pluto looking in at the window of the Practical Pig's house. Inside, the Three Little Pigs are singing and dancing on a rug made from the Big Bad Wolf. The card reads: "Sing a Christmas Carol! The Wolf is on the floor. And so, a Merry Christmas, and Hooray for '34!"

The 1937 card features the cast of Disney's first full-length feature film, *Snow White and the Seven Dwarfs*, which was premiered on 21 December 1937. This card has "Season's Greetings" embossed on the front and features a pastel illustration of Snow White, the Seven Dwarfs and others from the film. Because these characters were virtually unknown at the time, a small enclosure card, featuring Mickey, Minnie, Donald and Pluto, reads "and Greetings from us, too!" The card is now rarely found complete with the Mickey insert.

In the following year, the Studio favored an 8-page booklet format containing the poem, "T'was the Night Before Christmas," with appropriate changes.

It was the night before Christmas
And all thru the house
Not a creature is stirring
Except Mickey Mouse.

The booklet is illustrated with various Disney characters peacefully sleeping while Mickey wraps gifts. The last page shows two movie posters on a wall illuminated by a street light, one publicizing *Snow White and the Seven Dwarfs* (still playing in theaters around the world), the other announces the coming attraction, *Pinocchio*.

The Disney Studio also produced "fan cards," which were sent out to anyone who requested a photograph of their favorite Disney character. One such card features Mickey playing a piano, on top of which sits Minnie. The hand-colored card is inscribed "Sincerely yours, Mickey Mouse, Minnie Mouse and Walt Disney." Another features Mickey conducting the Three Little Pigs in concert while Pluto howls an accompaniment.

Not all Disney cards originated from the Studio. Kay Kamen's "Magic Movie Palette" Christmas card was sold to stores as a promotional give-away. The "mechanical" card had a double-sided printed wheel that simulated movie animation when turned rapidly. One side shows Mickey ice skating, the other, Minnie dancing in the snow.

Other card publishers included the White and Wyckoff Manufacturing Company of Holyoke, Massachusetts, which produced a range of Disney character greeting cards, among which was a novel "Talking" card.

Hall Brothers Inc. of Kansas City, Missouri, produced Hallmark Greeting Cards that featured Mickey Mouse. These included cards for every occasion — seasonal greeting cards, Valentine's

Day cards, congratulations cards, get well cards for the sick and birthday cards for both children and adults (page 158). The cards are die-cut shapes and retailed for 10 cents.

Germany was a leading producer of Valentine's Day cards, but by no means all of these were authorized. A number of publishers produced cards simply marked "Made in Germany."

During the early 1930s, various other types of cards were major features of the phenomenally successful Mickey Mouse

Clubs. These clubs issued not only membership cards, but club birthday cards, club pass cards and student honor cards.

Perhaps of all the commercially produced Mickey Mouse memorabilia the original movie posters, lobby posters and merchandise advertising posters are among the most desirable.

The first Mickey Mouse movie poster was produced in 1929. The poster shows a single image of Mickey in typical presentation pose, one hand on his hip and the other raised. Alongside, he is identified as "The World's Funniest Cartoon Character." Another simple, early poster shows Mickey Mouse strumming on a guitar, with lettering that announces "Mickey Mouse — Here Today!" Many were simply general posters that could be used to promote any Mickey Mouse cartoon. The title of the specific film was added later, in a white band provided for the purpose near the top or bottom of the poster.

A more elaborate poster, showing Mickey with a one-man band, advertises the Walt Disney cartoon *Mickey's Revue* (1932). A note in the lower right corner of the poster announces: "This advertising is the property of Columbia Pictures Corporation and is leased, not sold." The exhibitor is warned that he "must not trade, sell, give away or sublease it," and the poster had to be returned within 10 days after showing of the picture. Evidently, the poster would then be dispatched to another movie house playing that particular cartoon, and when the poster began to show wear and tear it was probably destroyed and replaced by Columbia. This helps to explain the rarity of posters of this kind.

However, there is more hope for the collector who is seeking lithographed Mickey Mouse store posters. These were produced to promote all kinds of merchandise. One colorful example is a 1937 poster promoting Mickey Mouse Cookies — "Wholesome . . . Delicious" — and a product of the National Biscuit Company. Many of these posters were boldly bright and featured high quality graphics.

Because so many posters were designed to be discarded after use, or simply became very worn, copies in prime condition are difficult to find. In consequence, they now command record prices at auction.

The movie posters illustrated here and on the following two pages represent the diversity of styles used on the posters produced for Disney films. Most of the animated shorts and all the feature films had special posters, and movie poster collecting is a specialized field. The most desirable are the posters for the pre-war animated features, although the very early (1928–30) generic Mickey Mouse posters may (in the late 1980s) command a price of several hundred dollars.

Wild Waves was released in 1929, when the cartoons were still described as "A Walt Disney comic, drawn by Ub Iwerks." The poster for the 1933 release *The Meller Drammer* depicts Mickey Mouse as Uncle Tom and Horace Horsecollar as Simon Legree in a production of "Uncle Tom's Cabin." *The Wayward Canary* was released in 1932, as was *The Whoopee Party*, one of Mickey's classic musical pictures, in which not only the guests but also the furniture and, eventually, the whole house get the beat and make whoopee.

Also released in 1932 was *Trader Mickey*, a pastiche of the much publicized 1931 MGM film *Trader Horn*, which was the first Hollywood picture to be filmed on location in Africa. The Walt Disney Archives.

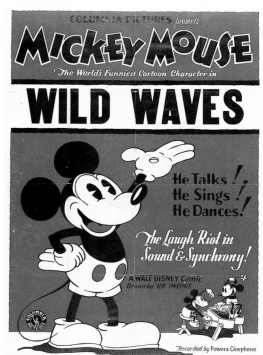

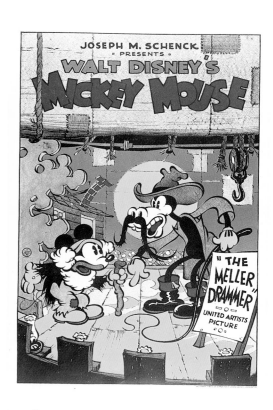

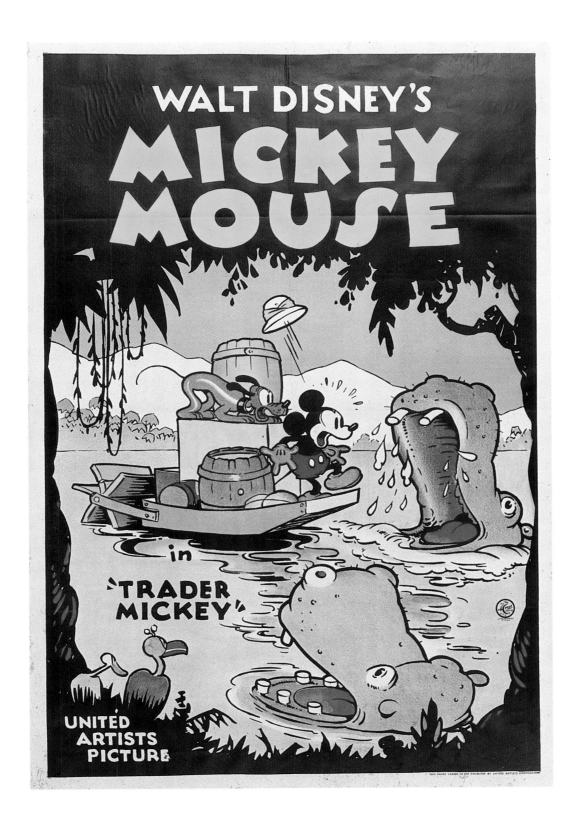

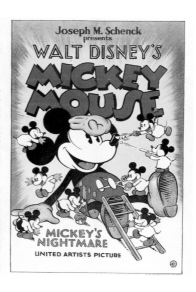

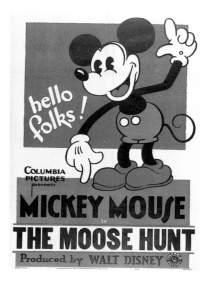

Touchdown Mickey was released in
1932, shortly after *Mickey's Nightmare*.
In *Mickey's Nightmare*, Mickey dreams of
marrying Minnie, but his sweet dream
turns into a nightmare when baby mice
appear on the scene.

  The Moose Hunt (1931) saw the first
appearance of Pluto, whom Mickey
accidentally "shoots" and then uses as a
"plane" when they are both chased over
a cliff by a moose.

  Building a Building, in which Mickey
saves Minnie from the over-passionate
advances of Peg Leg Pete, was released
in 1933, a year before *Ye Olden Days*,
the film that inspired the pop-up book
Mickey Mouse in King Arthur's Court (see
page 144). The Walt Disney Archives.

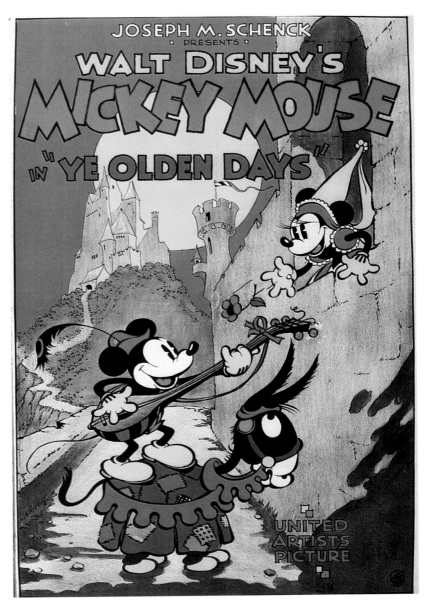

Illustrated here and opposite is a selection of early Mickey Mouse postcards, which were printed in England, France or Belgium. The leading manufacturer, printing Mickey cards as early as 1930, was the Inter-Art Company, England, which produced the three cards shown right above and some of those opposite. A similar type of card was printed by Woolstone Brothers, London, which identified its cards with the words "The Milton Post Card." After Britain, the second main source of postcards was Belgium, where manufacturers included Editions Feraille, W. Hogelbery A.G. and Colorart. It has not proved possible to identify the French manufacturers of the cards illustrated below right. No postcards by Valentine & Sons Ltd, which acquired a licence in 1935, are shown here: they are identifiable from the solid black oval eyes, for none of Valentine's cards show Mickey with pie-cut eyes. The Inter-Art cards shown here are all 5½ × 3½in (14 × 9cm). Right: Private Collection; below and opposite: The Robert Lesser Collection.

"Ain't I nice? And I'm still single!"

"If I had a talking picture of you-oo!"
Diese Musik ist für die Katz'!

"We'll be with you soon!"

and I'll be there with you, where my dreams come true!"

Mondscheinserenade!

"Am I making a hit with you?"

"Let's be as happy as we can all day long!"

Leckermäulchen!
"When I'm with you, Mickey, I'm near heaven!"

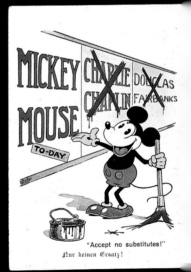

"Accept no substitutes!"
Nur keinen Ersatz!

In the early 1930s Hall Brothers, Inc., Kansas City, which later became Hallmark Greeting Cards and Hallmark, Inc., began the mass production of greeting cards for sale to the general public. The company created a complete range of Disney greeting cards for Christmas, birthdays and other occasions, from 1931 when they were first licensed. One series in the company's line featured cards that kept unfolding until they reached poster size! The birthday card shown here is 4in (10cm) square. The Bernard C. Shine Collection.

*Christmas Greetings
to Her Royal Highness Princess Elizabeth,
from Walter E. Disney, Hollywood.*

It is possible that Walt Disney sent this Christmas Card to Princess Elizabeth, the future Queen Elizabeth II. It is in an early 1931 Archive scrapbook and is postcard size, 5 × 7in (13 × 18cm). The Walt Disney Archives.

This paper Valentine's Day card (left) was made in the United States and was probably not licensed by Disney. It measures 5 × 3½in (13 × 9cm). The Bernard C. Shine Collection.

ORIGINAL ART

The idea of selling Disney animated film art was first suggested by Guthrie Sayle Courvoisier, a leading art connoisseur and owner of a fine art gallery in San Francisco. He correctly predicted that there was a market for this material in museums, university art departments and libraries, and that it would be sought by serious collectors of fine art and even interior designers. He approached Kay Kamen with the suggestion, and Kamen went ahead with a test marketing at Stix, Baer and Fuller department store, St Louis, Missouri without further involving Courvoisier. When Courvoisier learned of this, he wrote a polite letter of protest to Kamen, with copies to Walt and Roy Disney, emphasizing that this material belonged in the category of fine art, it was not merely a commercial commodity for the mass market.

Courvoisier's argument proved effective, and the test sales were stopped. To Kamen's credit, he accepted the Studio's decision with a good grace and later assisted Courvoisier in marketing the animated film art.

Courvoisier's first contract with Disney was restricted to the sale of "cels" from *Snow White and the Seven Dwarfs*. "Cels" are the paintings of animated figures on celluloid, thousands of which were rapidly changed over a static background painting to give the impression of continuous movement — an ingenious innovation first suggested by Earl Hurd in 1914.

Such was the success of Courvoisier's venture that the Disneys soon extended the dealer's rights to other cartoons and films, releasing a wider range of material. To the original cels were added some original backgrounds from the films, with or without the celluloid action figures superimposed, story board drawings (or story sketches) outlining the plot and original drawings executed by the leading animators. These original sketches and story board drawings are perhaps the most important of all because they most directly record the roots and development of Disney art. Although this material usually takes the form of no more than pencil or partly colored sketches, it epitomizes the creative energy and aesthetic dynamics being generated by the talented artists who worked in the Disney Studio during the early 1930s.

Cels are collectible because it took from 12 to 16 thousand of them to complete one seven-minute Mickey Mouse cartoon but, until Courvoisier stepped in, because of storage problems much of this original art was routinely destroyed by washing off the images once the film was completed so that the cel could be re-used. Nevertheless, some sketches and cels from the earlier cartoons were kept on file at the Studio for reference; others were kept by the animators for their own portfolios or given to friends and visitors to the Studio.

Occasionally, some of that material filters on to the market. For instance, in October 1981 Phillips Son & Neal, Inc. held an important auction of Disneyana that included collectibles from the estate of the late Al Taliaferro, who had been one of Disney's top comic-strip artists. Among the many items auctioned was a single cel of Mickey Mouse as the Sorcerer's Apprentice, which went for $1,400.00. There was also a four-panel, pen-and-ink Mickey Mouse daily strip drawn by Al Taliaferro dated 24 December 1934.

On 10 December 1984, the *Los Angeles Times* carried a report of a major sale of almost four hundred items of Disney animation art at Christie's East, New York. An astounding total of approximately $½ million was realized, some items exceeding the pre-sale estimate by as much as six times. Among the Mickey Mouse items of particular interest was a cake-and-icing covered Mickey celebrating his birthday. The top price went for Mickey Mouse swatting seven flies in one blow, as he appeared in *Brave Little Tailor* (1938). This cel with background sold for $20,900.

Black-and-white Mickey Mouse artwork is another very collectible area. Disney's leading artists produced the syndicated newspaper daily and Sunday comic strips, Ub Iwerks, arguably Disney's top animator, being just one outstanding contributor.

But here, a few words of caution. There are important storage considerations should you be fortunate enough to acquire any cels. Vintage cels were made of highly flammable cellulose nitrate, so original art from this period requires special handling. (After 1940, cels were no longer made of nitrate; acetate was used instead.) Apart from the possibility of combustion, cels stored in stacks may fuse together. Because the paint was applied in thick, opaque layers, chipping and flaking are also problems as the cel itself may shrink or wrinkle. Cels are best stored between sheets of glass, in a place where they will not be exposed to heat or humidity. The collector must also be cautious about forgeries, for it is possible now to produce very skilful copies of cels, so be at pains to ensure the authenticity of an item before buying such material.

The same caution applies in the case of black-and-white comic strips. Reproductions are easily made now. But there is a reliable means of authenticating such items. The originals usually have the copyright date and the syndicate's name glued to the lower right-hand corner.

Sotheby's, the New York auction house, now holds twice-yearly auctions of Disney collectibles where film cels are particularly sought after by three groups of buyers. The fine art connoisseurs and movie buffs are just as keen to snap up this work as the Mickey Mouse memorabilia collectors. If only Courvoisier's enterprise had started earlier.

These animation drawings for the 1936 cartoon *Thru the Mirror* were also used on the poster advertising the exhibition "Disney Animation and Animators" held at the Whitney Museum of American Art in 1981. The Walt Disney Archives.

This gouache on two celluloids applied to a Disney Studio master watercolor background of Mickey leading the band is from *The Band Concert* (1935), the first Mickey cartoon to be made in color. The cel measures 9 × 11¼in (23 × 28.5cm), and in December 1985 it realized a world record price of $24,000. The previous world record was $20,900 paid in 1984 for a cel of Mickey swatting flies from *Brave Little Tailor* (1938). The Walt Disney Company; courtesy Christie's, New York, and Dale Kelly, *Antique Toy World*.

COLLECTORS and COLLECTIONS

In every field of collecting, there are a few ardent enthusiasts who literally search the world to add to their collections. The people listed here all fall into that category, and it is thanks to their research and their collections that much information about the social history of Mickey Mouse merchandise has been garnered for posterity. Catalogues, personal letters and rare toys have come to light through their collecting zeal for the merchandise, both authorized and unauthorized, that was made between 1928 and 1938, the vintage years.

MEL BIRNKRANT

Birnkrant is interested in what he calls the "life force" of an item. "You would throw a piece of wood on to the fire, but if that piece of wood were carved in the image of a doll, you wouldn't dream of throwing it on to the fire," he explains. The doll has a magical essence of life.

Mickey Mouse is a fascinating and successful object because, although he is totally unrealistic, the little mouse, too, has an undeniable life force. Birnkrant elaborates: "The more life-imitating an object becomes, in the sense of resembling a living creature, the more it is a dead object. For example, the figures in a wax museum are more death-like than life-like. But Mickey, imitating neither mouse nor man, has a way of saying, 'I'm alive'."

A toy designer by profession, Birnkrant regards his Mickey merchandise as pieces of original art, even though each item was mass-produced. The craftsmen who designed the individual pieces were involved in the creation of a toy, regardless of how many copies were eventually produced. Each toy is one artist's interpretation of Mickey, and Birnkrant is more interested in the artist's interpretation than in the original form. He describes Mickey Mouse as basically consisting of just three circles, but they are circles that together form a very strong image. "What makes collecting Mickey Mouse interesting is this paradox: the image is indestructible, everybody who tackles it captures it, yet, capturing it, they miss it."

Birnkrant's collection attained its considerable size not only because he started earlier than other collectors, but because he continued to collect after many of them had stopped. He calls himself and other early collectors such as Ernest Trova, Richard Herker and John Fawcett, "explorers." Every Mickey piece that came into his collection was a real discovery. Birnkrant describes each item in his collection as "a souvenir, the residue of a great experience, such as the thrill of going to a Brimfield, Massachusetts, flea market at five o'clock in the morning with a flashlight — and finding a treasure."

Now that an increasing number of books and articles are being written about the Mickey Mouse merchandise, Birnkrant feels that collectors are being robbed of some of the enjoyment and excitement of those early discoveries. "Fate dictates what you are going to get," he says. Because so many different items were manufactured no one person could possibly get them all. "Every collector is going to get something that you are never going to have, and each collection, whatever its size, has its own character." Birnkrant is more impressed by small collections that have a few outstanding pieces than by vast collections that contain nothing he would like to find for himself.

He says there are now two criteria for judging a piece of Mickey Mouse merchandise. One is that you really like it because it is a great image. The other is that the piece is desirable. "In my own mind, I would like to say 'I love that thing even though I know it is common'," says Birnkrant. For him, the fun of being an early collector was in the pleasure of coming upon everything with a spontaneous reaction, without having to relate to its scarcity, desirability or who else wanted it.

His own collection began with a Mickey Mouse marionette given to him as a Christmas present by his wife after he had admired it in a store. Almost without realizing it, he began to acquire other items and was at first appalled when he discovered that he owned a thousand Mickey Mouse pieces. He felt that perhaps his interest had got "out of hand." Fortunately, a friend was able to reassure him that he had simply become a collector. His enthusiasm continued to grow — and so did his collection. Research indicates that in the 1930s Disney licensed over 50,000 different objects worldwide. Birnkrant says, "I would like them all."

ROBERT LESSER

Lesser is most interested in the vintage Mickey Mouse items that depict the "rat-faced Mickey." Because of their distance from California, overseas manufacturers of Disney toys had great freedom when designing early Mickey Mouse toys. The designers would go to see the cartoon films and then would create designs based on the quick sketches they had made. Because the toy makers of Nuremberg, Germany, perceived Mickey as a rat, many of these early toys have rat-like features.

"All of the early, great pieces are five fingered and have rat faces," says Lesser. "To my mind these are the most exciting pieces because they go back to *Steamboat Willie*," (the first of Mickey's films to be released).

According to the foreign toy manufacturers, the early Mickey drank booze and smoked cigars, and he is more exciting to Lesser than the "upright citizen" Mickey merchandise produced under the direct influence of Walt Disney. Collectors have discovered only a few of the items that were manufactured during those vintage years. "If collectors could go through every foreign newspaper of the 1930s, published in the weeks leading up to Christmas," Lesser claims, "they would discover advertisements for many, many toys in print that have never actually been found."

He explains that such a vast number of early Mickey Mouse toys was produced because "Mickey was eternally optimistic and optimism helped to make this creature the best salesman of the Depression era."

Talking of his own collection, Lesser recalls that when he was a student a professor told him: "Sooner or later something in life is going to get you, be careful of what it is!" The "thing" that got Lesser turned out to be collecting. He describes two major categories of collectors: long-distance runners and short-distance "sweaters," and he considers himself one of the former. The passion of the short-distance collector is intense, steamy and short lived, burning itself out in about six months. When the burn-out occurs, the short-distance collector realizes the insanity of what he is doing and promptly sells his collection. The long-distance runner, on the other hand, maintains his interest in collecting by virtue of a special vision that enables him to see the quality in graphic art design and in what he collects. He sees things that few other people see, because he is a visual person. He collects until the day he dies.

Besides these two groups of collectors, there are those who only want to buy cheaply and are so price conscious that they build vast collections of "garbage." And there are still a rare few who assemble a relatively small collection of superb pieces. "This type of collector refines his collection, perhaps even throwing away his mistakes, until only the best remain," says

Lesser. Like the obsessive gambler, no matter what the cost, this collector must find the necessary money to buy the piece he covets. Eventually, he has to choose between the collection and everything else in life.

BERNARD C. SHINE

The graphic art form of the pieces is what attracted Shine to collecting Mickey Mouse merchandise. It has everything good graphic art should have: color, form and dimension, with the bonus of animation. The toys move and are "alive." According to Shine, this art form is very direct: it is understandable and touchable, and therefore has a certain playful intimacy. At the same time, Mickey Mouse has a symbolism and significance that is almost mystical and magical. As a creature of fantasy, he has a lasting power over the collector.

"The reason the 1930s Mickey has such tremendous charisma has something to do with the primitiveness of the animation at that period," explains Shine. Walt Disney and Ub Iwerks, the first Mickey Mouse animator, were in their twenties when Mickey was created around 1928. In his first 10 years, he had a youthful brilliance. He was not yet an American institution, just a comic character who could do and act as he pleased. He could be daring, bold, even brash. Disney and Iwerks were still experimenting, developing and changing the character. "The real excitement of the early Mickey was that he had not yet matured, he was pure," says Shine. "I'm quite fond of the early character and as Mickey evolved and found himself, he lost me. There is a certain excitement and brilliance about any prototype."

Because of the appeal that these early qualities exercise over him, Bernard Shine limits his collection to items made before 1940, but it is nevertheless broadbased. With a preference for sculptural figures, Shine also collects Mickey advertising art, buttons, brooches, other jewelry, watches, games, books and paper items. He says, "I like the graphics, no matter what the form."

He has also limited his collecting interest to Mickey Mouse and his immediate circle. Mickey was the leading character, the star of the Disney Studio. According to Shine, Mickey always active, and Minnie was always observing, admiring and pointing out these activities. He wishes that the material had no monetary value because, even though this would render his own collection valueless, he would rather think of it as making an aesthetic statement. Unlike most collectible items, Mickey Mouse worked his way up the social ladder. Starting as an item found in rummage store sales and flea markets, Mickey now appears on the prestigious auction floors of Sotheby', Christie's and Phillips.

Shine started collecting when he was in college. His first acquisition was a pair of Mickey Mouse watches that he bought from a second-hand jewelry store. Later, he sold them because he thought it was foolish to own something so "trivial," only to discover that he mourned their absence. In his search for replacements, he discovered other items that became the foundation of his collection. It was as if the Mickey Mouse items had an "energy force," and Shine formed an emotional attachment to each one. "I think one of the reasons I collect something so absurd, so trivial, ridiculous and meaningless to most of the world, is because I need the fantasy to escape from my otherwise serious profession," says Shine, who is a lawyer.

The only character to approach Mickey in popularity was Donald Duck, and he was not created unti 1934. Mickey was being mass produced in 1930. Disney described Donald as the "Clark Gable of our stable," because of his great appeal. He was given the freedom to live life as if no one were watching, while Mickey evolved into more of a symbol than a character. According to Shine, people could identify with Donald because there is a little of his irascible personality in all of us. He adds, "Perhaps, if Donald had never been created, Mickey Mouse would have continued to have that kind of freedom."

STEFAN RAIA SZTYBEL

Stefan regards collecting Mickey Mouse merchandise items as a "constant compulsion to acquire more and more of Mickey." He wants to be surrounded by thousands of the same mouse images because "the more you have of the same image, the easier it is to get a psychedelic effect of movement, simply by

scanning with your eyes." Stefan recalls that initially he thought that his collection of Mickey Mouse merchandise was going to be perceived as childish. He was therefore surprised by the actual reaction: "At last, you're doing something serious."

Mickey Mouse has always been Stefan's "big super-hero," and when the *Mickey Mouse Club* was shown on television in the late 1950s, he watched faithfully every day. It was at this time that he discovered he liked the pre-1940s cartoons best.

In the 1960s, when the nostalgia craze started, Stefan customarily presented a modern Mickey Mouse item to his friends as a gift when an occasion arose. On Stefan's thirtieth birthday his friends reciprocated with a party at which they all gave *him* Mickey Mouse gifts. "So there I sat, with an assortment of things that were very much like the things I'd given out for years," says Stefan. On looking into the faces of these items, he realized that none of them was the real Mickey Mouse. Stefan determined to find a true Mickey Mouse image and, starting with toys shops and Woolworth stores, he eventually carried his search to flea markets and collectors' toy shows.

Stefan finally tracked down his first Knickerbocker Mickey Mouse and, faced with the reality of the high prices paid for good old toys, he anxiously carried off his prize. He recalls. "I was so nervous with this thing in the brown paper bag, this icon, that I jumped into a taxi cab and returned home." That was the beginning of his love for the classic figure of Mickey Mouse.

Having avoided economics at school, Stefan soon learned the basic principles of supply and demand when he became a Mickey Mouse collector. Dealing directly with people who have something you want, or who want something you have, increases your business acumen tremendously. Previously, Stefan had never been able to save or invest money, but spurred by his new interest, he has built up valuable equity in the form of his collection. "Being a nonconformist, I was always something of an outsider, but I find collecting has brought me into, and made me more acceptable to, the mainstream culture in this country. Who could put Mickey Mouse down?" concludes Stefan. Who, indeed.

Mel Birnkrant is pictured here with the wooden figures of Mickey and Minnie sculpted for a French carousel (see also page 90). Photograph by Jim Munsie.

The assorted mice (right) are from Mel Birnkrant's collection; the display measures 12 × 28in (30 × 71cm).

Surrounded by Mickey heads from his extensive collection is Bernard C. Shine. Photograph by Eric Sander.

In his small apartment in New York Robert Lesser (right) sits surrounded by his collection, which includes everything related to American comic memorabilia from early Mickey Mouse toys, Felix the Cat, Betty Boop to Popeye. He has been collecting for 20 years.

Ward and Betty Kimball in their orange grove, San Gabriel, California. The wooden Mickey Mouse table and Pluto bench are very rare items. The table, which is 26in (66cm) high, 22in (56cm) wide and 27in (69cm) long, has Mickey holding up one end and Minnie the other. The bench, 15in (38cm) high and 21½in (55cm) long, has Pluto's head and front at one end and his tail at the other. They were made in 1934–5 by Kroehler, a subsidiary of Atlas Development Co., Ltd, Richmond, California. Betty and Ward are holding their Charlotte Clark dolls, which are also pictured on page 80.

Betty and Ward Kimball both worked at the Disney Studio, and their identification cards are shown below. Each card is 2½ × 3½in (6 × 9cm), and they were signed by A.G. Keener, who was treasurer at the Studio at the time. On the backs of the cards are the words: "Employee is to sign Identification Card, and if required, must present for identification." Ward's card is number 214 and Betty's is number 99. The Ward Kimball Collection.

BIBLIOGRAPHY

Abrams, Robert and Canemaker, John, *Treasures of Disney Animation Art,* Abbeville Press, New York, 1982

Bailey, Adrian, *Walt Disney's World of Fantasy,* Everest House, New York/Paper Tiger, London, 1982

Bain, David and Harris, Bruce (editors), *Mickey Mouse: Fifty Happy Years,* Crown Publishers Inc., New York/New English Library, London, 1978

Feild, Robert D., *The Art of Walt Disney,* Macmillan, New York, 1942; William Collins, London and Glasgow, 1947

Finch, Christopher, *The Art of Walt Disney: From Mickey Mouse to the Magic Kingdoms,* Harry N. Abrams Inc., New York, 1981

Heide, Robert and Gilman, John, *Cartoon Collectibles,* Doubleday & Co., New York, 1983

Holliss, Richard and Sibley, Brian (editors), *Mickey Mouse: His Life and Times,* Harper & Row, New York/Fleetway Books, London, 1986

Lesser, Robert, *A Celebration of Comic Art and Memorabilia,* Hawthorn Books Inc., New York, 1975

Maltin, Leonard, *The Disney Films,* Crown Publishers Inc., New York, 1973

Munsey, Cecil, *Disneyana,* Hawthorn Books Inc., New York, 1974

O'Brien, Flora (editor), *Donald Duck: 50 Years of Happy Frustration,* HPBooks Inc., Tucson, Arizona/Three Duck Editions, London, 1984

—,—, *Goofy: The Good Sport,* HPBooks Inc., Tucson, Arizona/Ebury Press, London, 1985

Overstreet, Robert M., *The Comic Book Price Guide volume 13,* Overstreet Publications, Cleveland, 1983

Peary, Gerald and Peary, Danny (editors), *The American Animated Cartoon: A Critical Anthology,* E.P. Dutton, New York, 1980

Rublowsky, John and Heyman, Kenneth, *Pop Art,* Basic Books, New York, 1965

Shine, Bernard C., *Mickey Memories from the Vintage Years,* unpublished thesis

Taylor, Deems, *Walt Disney's Fantasia* (Foreword by Leopold Stokowski), Simon & Schuster, New York, 1940

Thomas, Frank and Johnston, Ollie, *Disney Animation – The Illusion of Life,* Abbeville Press, New York, 1981

Tombusch, Tom, *Tomart's Illustrated Disneyana Catalog and Price Guide* (3 volumes), Tomart Publications, Dayton, Ohio, 1985

Waugh, Coulton, *The Comics,* Macmillan, New York, 1947

Articles

Carr, Harry, "The Only Unpaid Movie-Star", *American Magazine,* March 1931

Disney, Walt, "Merry Christmas, Mickey and Minnie Mouse", *Delineator,* December 1932

Johnston, Alva, "Mickey Mouse", *Woman's Home Companion,* July 1934

Miller, Diane Disney, "My Dad, Walt Disney", *Saturday Evening Post,* 17 November 1956

Skolsky, Sidney, "Mickey Mouse", *Cosmopolitan* Magazine, February 1934

Syring, Richard H., "One of the Great", *Silver Screen* Magazine, November 1932

"Walt Disney, A Biography"; "Animated Cartoon World of Walt Disney"; "Animated Feature Length World of Walt Disney"; The Art of Animation"; "Live Action Movie-World of Walt Disney"; "Disneyland" and "Wisdom of Walt Disney"; *Wisdom* Magazine volume 32, December 1959

"Mickey Mouse, the First Fifty Years", Catalogue, Department of Film of the Museum of Modern Art, New York, 1978

Hake's Americana and Collectibles

BISQUEOGRAPHY

CHARACTER(S)	HEIGHT IN INCHES (mm)	NUMBER INCISED ON FIGURINE	DESCRIPTION	CHARACTER(S)	HEIGHT IN INCHES (mm)	NUMBER INCISED ON FIGURINE	DESCRIPTION
1. Mickey	1¼ (32)	None	Waving with right hand; the smallest Mickey bisque	21. Mickey	3¼ (83)	None	Bulbous figure holding song book; white feet
2. Mickey	1½ (38)	None	Waving with right hand	22. Mickey	3¼ (83)	None	Bulbous figure playing accordion; white feet
3. Mickey	1¾ (44)	None	Right hand on hip; left hand down by side	23. Mickey	3¼ (83)	None	Bulbous figure playing banjo; white feet
4. Mickey	1⅞ (48) (3¼ (83) long)	None	Riding in canoe	24. Mickey	3¼ (83)	None	Bulbous figure playing French horn; white feet
5. Mickey	2¾ (70)	None	Two movable arms	25. Mickey	3¼ (83)	None	Bulbous figure playing drum; white feet
6. Mickey	2¾ (70)	S504	Hands on hips	26. Mickey	3¾ (95)	C72	Playing snare drum
7. Mickey	2¾ (70)	S442	Sitting position	27. Mickey	3¾ (95)	C73	Playing French horn
8. Mickey	3¾ (95)	S15	Holding flag in right hand; left hand on sword to side	28. Mickey	3¾ (95)	S1390	Nodding head attached to body with cord
9. Mickey	3¼ (83)	S16	Holding sword in right hand; left hand to side	29. Mickey	3¾ (95)	S177	Wearing hat and holding cane
10. Mickey	3¼ (83)	S17	Holding rifle to side and wearing ammo packs; head turned slightly to right	30. Mickey	4 (102)	S33	Wearing hat and holding cane
11. Mickey	3¼ (83)	S492	Holding rifle	31. Mickey	4 (102)	None	In tuxedo; holding top hat and cane
12. Mickey	2⅜ (60)	S26?	Wearing baseball glove on left hand	32. Mickey	4 (102)	S1277	Wearing nightgown
13. Mickey	2⅜ (60)	?	Wearing baseball glove on left hand and holding baseball in right hand	33. Mickey	4½ (114)	A567	Standing next to garbage can
14. Mickey	2⅜ (60)	?	Holding baseball bat	34. Mickey	4¾ (121)	None	Bulbous head; two movable arms; believed to be the first Mickey bisque ever made
15. Mickey	2⅜ (60)	?	Wearing catcher's gear and holding catcher's mit	35. Mickey	5¼ (133)	None	Standing on green platform; hands on hips
16. Mickey	3¼ (83)	S64	Wearing baseball glove on left hand	36. Mickey	5¼ (133)	A116	Hands on hips
17. Mickey	3¼ (83)	S65	Wearing baseball glove on left hand and holding baseball in right hand	37. Mickey	5 (127)	None	Single figure toothbrush holder; bulbous head; right arm straight and movable
18. Mickey	3¼ (83)	S66	Holding baseball bat	38. Mickey	5 (127)	None	Single figure toothbrush holder; head turned to left; right arm straight and movable
19. Mickey	3¼ (83)	S67	Wearing catcher's gear and holding catcher's mit				
20. Mickey	3¼ (83)	None	Bulbous figure holding conductor's baton; two movable arms; white feet				

CHARACTER(S)	HEIGHT IN INCHES (mm)	NUMBER INCISED ON FIGURINE	DESCRIPTION
39. Mickey	5 (127)	C103	Single figure toothbrush holder; head turned to left; right arm slightly curved and movable
40. Mickey	5 (127)	None	Two movable arms
41. Mickey	5¾ (146)	C106	Two movable arms
42. Mickey	5¼ (133)	None	Playing accordion
43. Mickey	5¼ (133)	None	Playing French horn
44. Mickey	5¼ (133)	None	Playing banjo
45. Mickey	5¼ (133)	None	Playing drum
46. Mickey	5¾ (146)	S36	Playing French horn
47. Mickey	7½ (191)	S509	Standing on green base; two movable arms
48. Mickey	8¾ (222)	None	Standing on green base; two movable arms; the largest Mickey bisque
49. Minnie	2¾ (70)	S505	Hands on hips
50. Minnie	2¾ (70)	S443	Sitting position
51. Minnie	3¼ (83)	S18	Holding nurse's kit in right hand next to right leg; left hand on chest
52. Minnie	3¼ (83)	S493	Holding nurse's kit under right arm; left hand on hip
53. Minnie	3½ (89)	C69	Playing mandolin
54. Minnie	3½ (89)	C71	Playing accordion
55. Minnie	3½ (89)	S424	Pushing wheelbarrow, used as pincushion
56. Minnie	3¾ (95)	S178	Wearing hat and holding umbrella and purse
57. Minnie	4 (102)	S34	Wearing hat and holding umbrella and purse
58. Minnie	4 (102)	S1276	Wearing nightgown
59. Minnie	5 (127)	None	Standing next to garbage can
60. Minnie	5 (127)	None	Standing on green platform; hands on hips
61. Minnie	5¼ (133)	A117	Hands on hips
62. Minnie	5 (127)	None	Single figure toothbrush holder; bulbous head; right arm straight and movable
63. Minnie	5 (127)	None	Single figure toothbrush holder; head turned to right; left arm straight and movable
64. Minnie	5¼ (133)	C104	Single figure toothbrush holder; head turned to right; left arm slightly curved and movable
65. Minnie	5 (127)	None	Two movable arms
66. Minnie	6 (152)	C105	Two movable arms
67. Minnie	5½ (140)	S3B	Playing violin
68. Pluto	3¼ (83)	S433	Seated next to guard house
69. Pluto	2¼ (57)	None	Sitting position
70. Pluto	2¾ (70)	S35	Sitting position
71. Donald	1¾ (44)	M-1	Head turned to his right; hands on hips
72. Donald	3 (76)	3	Bill open; hands to sides
73. Donald	3¾ (95)	S1333	Holding flag
74. Donald	3 (76)	S1334	Holding bugle
75. Donald	3 (76)	S1335	Holding rifle
76. Donald	3 (76)	S1336	Holding sword
77. Donald	3¼ (83)	None	Walking; bill in air
78. Donald	3¼ (83)	1	Sitting on rocking horse
79. Donald	3¼ (83)	2	Sitting on scooter
80. Donald	3¼ (83)	3	Standing on scooter
81. Donald	3 (76)	None	In admiral's hat and coat
81a. Donald	3 (76) (4¾ (121) long)	None	Riding in canoe
82. Donald	4 (102)	???	Two movable arms; mid-size bill
83. Donald	4¼ (108)	S1132	Toothbrush holder; two Donalds — Siamese twins

CHARACTER(S)	HEIGHT IN INCHES (mm)	NUMBER INCISED ON FIGURINE	DESCRIPTION
84. Donald	4½ (114)	S1278	Hands on hips
85. Donald	4 (102)	None	Holding paintbrush and can of paint
86. Donald	4 (102)	S1158	Playing mandolin
87. Donald	4 (102)	S1130	Playing violin
88. Donald	4 (102)	S1131	Playing accordion
89. Donald	4½ (114)	S1130	Playing violin
90. Donald	4½ (114)	S1131	Playing accordion
91. Donald	4¾ (121)	None	Toothbrush holder; standing next to a pillar
92. Donald	5¼ (133)	None	Toothbrush holder; profile of Donald looking to right
93. Donald	5¾ (146)	S1128	Two movable arms
94. The Goof	1¾ (44)	None	Right hand in back; left hand to side
95. The Goof	3½ (89)	None	Right hand in back; left hand to side
96. Horace	1⅞ (48)	None	Hands to side
97. Horace	3¾ (95)	None	Hands to side
98. Horace	5 (127)	None	Arms folded across chest
99. Clarabelle	5 (127)	None	Hands on dress
100. Mickey and Pluto	2¼ (57)	None	Mickey riding Pluto
101. Mickey and Donald	1⅞ (48) (3¼ (83) long)	None	Riding in canoe
102. Mickey, Minnie and Pluto	3½ (89)	S335	Toothbrush holder; seated on sofa
103. Mickey and Pluto	4½ (114)	None	Toothbrush holder; Mickey washing Pluto's face
104. Mickey, Minnie and Donald	4½ (114)	S1354	Toothbrush holder; Donald's arms around Mickey and Minnie
105. Mickey and Minnie	4¾ (121)	C100	Toothbrush holder; standing side-by-side
106. Mickey and Minnie	5½ (140)	S178	Mickey and Pluto side-by-side; Mickey's right arm movable

Note:
Question marks ("?") above indicate either an unknown or illegible number incised on figurine.

This list is limited to Japanese painted bisque figurines of Mickey, Minnie, Pluto, Donald, The Goof, Horace and Clarabelle. It does not include: (1) Japanese glazed figurines, (2) figurines from any other country of origin, or (3) figurines of Disney characters other than those listed above.

Bisque 81a was discovered by the author subsequent to his original compilation of this Bisqueography in 1982.

© 1982 Bernard C. Shine

U.S. DISNEY MERCHANDISE LICENSEES 1930–8

Acme Underwear Co. — *pajamas*
Adler Favor & Novelty Co., Inc. — *favors*
Alexander Doll Co. — *dolls*
C.S. Allen Corp. — *candy*
S.L. Allen & Co., Inc. — *sleds*
Aluminum Specialty Co. — *toy kitchenware*
American Hard Rubber Co. — *combs*
American Latex Corp. — *rubber pants*
American Lithographic Co. — *school tablets*
American Merri-Lei Corp. — *party goods*
American Toy Works — *games*
The Amloid Co. — *baby toys*
O.B. Andrews Co. — *playhouses*
Apon Novelty Co. — *novelties*
Artisto, Inc. — *framed pictures*
Athletic Shoe Co. — *moccasins*
Atlas Development Co. (Kroehler) — *furniture*
Automatic Recording Safe Co. — *banks*
Bachmann Brothers, Inc. — *plastic toys*
Banner Brothers, Inc.
    Kiddie Kit (also Columbia Products Corp.)
Barmon Brothers Co. — *clothing*
Bates Art Industries — *framed pictures*
Behrend & Rothschild — *banks*
Arthur Beir & Co., Inc. — *fabrics*
Irving Berlin, Inc. — *sheet music*
Bernstein Sons Shirt Corp. — *shirts*
Berst-Forster-Dixfield Co. — *paper products*
Bibo and Lang, Inc. — *books*
H. &. J. Block — *coats*
Blue Ribbon Books, Inc. — *books*
George Borgfeldt & Co. — *toys*
Milton Bradley Co. — *games*
Brandle & Smith Co. — *candy*
Brayton's Laguna Pottery — *figurines*
Brier Manufacturing Co. — *jewelry*
Brown & Bigelow — *calendars*
Bryant Electric Co. — *dishes*
Irving Caesar — *sheet music*
Capitol Cravat Co. — *neckware*
Caproni Galleries Inc. — *plaster figures*
Cartier, Inc. — *jewelry*

Hugh Chalmers, Jr. — *bouncing toys*
Character Art Manufacturing Co., Inc. — *thermometers*
Chicago Art Needle Works Co. — *needlework*
Kay Christy of California — *clothing*
Charlotte Clark — *dolls*
Joseph H. Clark — *hosiery*
Clopay Corp. — *dolls, etc.*
Cohn & Rosenberger — *jewelry*
Cohn-Hall-Marx — *printed cottons*
Colcombet-Werk, Inc. — *silk fabrics*
Colgate-Palmolive-Peet Co. — *soap packaging*
Collins-Kirk, Inc. — *cut-outs*
The Colson Co. — *tricycles*
Comfort Slipper Co. — *slippers*
Commonwealth Toy and Novelty Co. — *toys*
Cone Export & Commission Co. — *fabrics*
Consolidated Biscuit Co. — *suckers*
Continental Cushion Spring Co. — *chairs*
Continental Undergarment Co., Inc. — *underwear*
Converse Rubber Co. — *shoes*
Floyd L. Cooper — *jewelry*
Michael Cooper — *robes*
Courvoisier Galleries — *artwork*
Crawford Furniture Mfg. Co. — *furniture, etc.*
Crown Novelty Co., Inc. — *curtains*
The Crown Overall Mfg. Co. — *clothing*
Crown Toy Mfg. Co., Inc. — *banks, dolls*
Curtiss Candy Co. — *candy*
Cypress Novelty Corp. — *birthday candles*
Davis & Holly, Inc. — *stationery*
The Dayton Toy and Specialty Co. — *wheel toys*
Dell Publishing Co., Inc. — *comics*
Dennison Mfg. Co. — *party supplies*
Theodore Diamond, Inc. — *mirrors*
Joseph Dixon Crucible Co. — *pencil boxes*
Dolly Toy Co. — *toys*
David D. Doniger and Co. — *sweaters*
Doris Lamp Shades, Inc. — *lamp shades*
Draper-Maynard Co. — *sporting goods*
Jack Dubin Mfg. Co. — *hats*
Helen Hughes Dulany — *trays*
Einson-Freeman Co. — *masks, games*
Eisendrath Glove Co. — *gloves*
Ely & Walker Dry Goods Co. — *dresses*
Emerson Radio & Phonograph Corp. — *radios*
Empire Products Corp. — *popcorn popper*
Etched Products Corp. — *matchbox holders*

Everett Pulp & Paper Co. — *paper products*
Fallani & Cohn, Inc. — *table cloths*
Farm Crest Bakeries — *cookies*
Fine Art Pictures — *wall decorations*
Fine Infants Dress Co., Inc. — *dresses*
Fisch & Co., Inc. — *clothing*
A. S. Fischbach, Inc. — *costumes*
Fisher-Price Toys, Inc. — *pull-toys*
Fleischaker & Baum — *dolls*
G. H. & E. Freyberg, Inc. — *stamped materials*
Friedberger-Aaron Mfg. Co. — *wash cloths*
Fulton Specialty Co. — *rubber stamps*
Galax Mirror Co. — *mirrors*
General Foods Corp. — *cereal boxes*
General Ribbon Mills, Inc. — *ribbons*
Germain Seed & Plant Co. — *seeds*
Geuder, Paeschke & Frey Co. — *lunch kit*
I. Ginzkey-Maffersdorf, Inc. — *baby blankets*
Glaser-Crandell Co. — *jam jars*
Glenn Confections, Inc. — *chewing gum*
Gotham Pressed Steel Corp. — *cleaning sets*
Graham Mfg. Co. — *giftwrap*
Grosset & Dunlap, Inc. — *books*
Gum, Inc. — *chewing gum*
Hales Pictures, Inc. — *poster pictures*
Hall Brothers, Inc. — *greeting cards*
Halsam Products Co. — *blocks*
Hamilton Enterprises, Inc. — *candy vendor*
Hamilton Metal Products Co. — *tool boxes*
Henry Heide, Inc. — *candy*
Herbert Hosiery Mills, Inc. — *hosiery*
Herrmann Handkerchief Co., Inc. — *handkerchiefs*
Herz & Kory — *pocketbooks*
Hickok Mfg. Co., Inc. — *belts*
A. Stein Hickory & Co. — *clothing*
N. N. Hill Brass Co. — *pull toys*
Hollywood Film Enterprises — *film*
Home Foundry Mfg. Co. — *molds*
Hal Horne, Inc. — *magazine*
Hughes-Autograf Brush Co., Inc. — *brushes*
Henry L. Hughes Co., Inc. — *toothbrushes*
Ideal Aeroplane & Supply Co., Inc. — *toy planes*
Ideal Novelty & Toy Co. — *dolls*
The Imperial Knife Co. — *pocket knives*
Ingersoll-Waterbury Co. — *timepieces*
Inkograph Company, Inc. — *pens*
International Latex Corp. — *baby products*

Company	Product
International Silver Co.	silverware
H. Jacob & Sons, Inc.	footwear
Johnson & Johnson	game
K. K. Publications	magazine
Kay Kamen, Ltd.	promo items
Max Kasnowitz & Sons	purses
Ira G. Katz	hats
Julius Katz & Co., Inc.	clothing
The Kaynee Co.	clothing
Robert Kayton	garden kit
Kenilworth Press, Inc.	games
Kerk Guild, Inc.	wall plaques
Keystone Mfg. Co.	movie projectors
Kilgore Manufacturing Co.	toys
King Features Syndicate, Inc.	comic strips
King Innovations, Inc.	purses
Knickerbocker Toy Co., Inc.	dolls
Richard G. Krueger, Inc.	chinaware, etc.
Kurlash Co.	scissors
Philip Labe	table covers, etc.
LaMode Studios, Inc.	lamps
The Lander Co. Inc.	perfume
Langer Knitting Mills, Inc.	sweaters
Lapin-Kurley Kew, Inc.	hair ornaments
Libbey Glass Co.	glasses
Lightfoot-Schultz Co.	soap
The Lionel Corp.	toy trains
Loomtogs, Inc.	clothing
Lorraine Novelty Mfg. Co., Inc.	purses
Joseph Love, Inc.	dresses
Ludford Fruit Products Co.	beverages
McCall Co.	patterns
David McKay Publishing Co.	books
A. Mclean & Son	candy
Magill-Weinsheimer Co.	poster stamps
Manhattan Soap Co.	soap
Marks Brothers Co.	toys
Louis Marx & Co.	mechanical toys
May Fair Togs, Inc.	snow suits
May Hosiery Mills	hosiery
May Knitting Co., Inc.	sweaters
The Mengel Co.	playthings
The Metal Ware Corp.	toy stoves
The Meyercord Co.	decals
Micro-lite Co., Inc.	lights
Milko Cone and Baking Co., Inc.	cones
Miller Corsets, Inc.	corsets
Monroe Luggage Co., Inc.	cases
Movie Jecktor Co., Inc.	projectors
Moviescope Corp.	flip books
Murray Knitwear Co.	sweaters
Mutual-Sunset Lamp Mfg. Co.	lamps
Nashua Mfg. Company	linens
National Biscuit Company	cookies
National Dairy Products	dairy products
Naylor Corporation	hand-crafts
Neher-Whitehead & Co.	bottle collars
Thomas Nelson & Sons	books
Louis Nessel & Co., Inc.	linens
D. H. Neumann Company	clothing
Nevins Drug Co.	toothpaste
Noble & Cooley Company	musical instruments
Noblitt-Sparks Industries, Inc.	radios
Noma Electric Corporation	Christmas lights
Norwich Knitting Company	children's clothing
Notions, Inc.	notions
Oak Rubber Company	balloons
Odora Company, Inc.	toy chests
Ohio Art Company	metal toys
Old King Cole, Inc.	window display items
Olympia Knitting Mills, Inc.	knitted wear
E. and A. Opler, Inc.	cocoa malt flavoring
Overland Candy Corporation	candy
Owens-Illinois Can Company	containers
Owens-Illinois Glass Company	drinking glasses
Owens-Illinois Pacific Coast Co.	glass containers
Paas Dye Company	egg decorations
A.G. Palmer Supply Company	party favors
Palmer Brothers Company	bedspreads and drapes
Paper Novelty Mfg. Co.	Valentine Day cards
Para Mfg. Co., Inc.	shower curtains
Paris Neckwear Co., Inc.	boyswear
Parker Brothers	games
The Peerless Smoking Jacket Co., Inc.	robes and beachwear
The Pepsodent Company	toothpaste
Philadelphia Badge Co.	badges and buckles
Leo F. Phillips Co., Inc.	dress buttons
Pictorial Products Co.	toilet soap
Piqua Hosiery Company, Inc.	sport shirts
Plastic Novelties, Inc.	pencil sharpeners, etc.
The Platt & Munk Company, Inc.	slate
Pontiac Spring and Bumper Co.	toys
Powers Paper Company	stationery
Printowel Corporation	towels
Procter & Gamble	paper masks
Pyramid Leather Goods Company	children's handbags
R.C.A. Victor Corporation	records
Florence Reichman, Inc.	hats
Philip Reiter, Inc.	jewelry
Reliance Picture Frame Co.	framed pictures
Irving W. Rice	soap statuettes
The Richmond School Furniture Co.	blackboards
Rock Run Mills, Inc.	crib covers
Roff Knitting Mills	clothing
William Rogers & Son	silverware
Ross and Ross	dolls
Saalfield Publishing Co.	books
Sackman Brothers Company	costumes
The Salem China Company	chinaware
Henry Schanzer and Sons, Inc.	sweaters
Joseph Schneider, Inc.	wind-up toy
John F. Schoener, Inc.	candy
A. H. Schreiber Company, Inc.	underwear
Schumann China Corporation	chinaware
Scott and Bowne	booklet
Seiberling Latex Products Co.	rubber toys
Seneca Textile Corporation	piece goods
Service Industries, Inc.	masonite cut-outs
Sherman Bros. Rainwear Corp.	raincoats
Philip Shlansky and Bro. Inc.	suits and coats
M. Slifka & Sons	leather belts
Sloan & Company	jewelry
Alexander Smith & Sons Carpet Co.	carpets and rugs
Smith, Hogg & Co., Inc.	linens
Smith and Peters	candy
Foster D. Snell Sales Corp.	cigarette snappers
Soreng-Manegold Company	lamps, etc.
Southern Dairies, Inc.	dairy products
Speidel Corporation	costume jewelry
Standard Brief Case Co., Inc.	briefcases
Standard Oiled Clothing Co., Inc.	raincoats
Stark Brothers Ribbon Corporation	ribbons
Stationers Specialty Corporation	blotters
Margarete Steiff & Co., Inc.	stuffed dolls
A. Stein and Co.	baby clothes
Barney Stempler & Sons, Inc.	hangers
Stonite Company, Inc.	door stops
Storkline Furniture Corporation	juvenile furniture
The Straits Corp.	toys
Sun Oil Company (Sunoco)	ads

Swift & Company	*flower seeds*
Thomas P. Taylor Company	*clothing*
Telemovie Co.	*film*
Texas Star Flour Mills	*flour bags*
Thorens, Inc.	*Swiss music boxes*
Charles Tobias Bro. & Co.	*hats and caps*
Toy Kraft Company	*wooden toys*
Toy Tinkers, Inc.	*pictures*
Trifari, Krussman & Fishel, Inc.	*novelty jewelry*
Trojan Maid, Inc.	*clothes*
Troy Sunshade Co.	*carrier bags*
Truitt Brothers, Inc.	*shoes*
United Biscuit Co. of America	*crackers and biscuits*
United Wall Paper Factories	*wallpaper borders*
U.S. Electric Mfg. Corp.	*flashlights*
U.S. Lock & Hardware Co.	*jack sets*
Valentine Textile Corp.	*cloth*
Vogue Needlecrafts Company	*stenciled needlecraft*
Volupte, Inc.	*compacts, etc.*
Volz & Fawcett	*handkerchiefs*
Waldburger, Tanner & Co.	*handkerchiefs*
Rolf Wallach	*imported scarfs*
Louis Weiss	*rainwear, etc.*
Western Art Leather Company	*souvenir pillows*
White and Whyckoff Mfg. Co.	*stationery*
Whitman Publishing Co.	*books*
Wilbur-Suchard Chocolate Company	*candy*
William Rogers & Son	*silverware*
Rollin Wilson Co.	*archery sets*
Bernhard Wolf	*handkerchiefs*
Woodhaven Metal Stamping Company, Inc.	*toy sweepers*
Wornova Mfg. Co.	*costumes*
J. L. Wright, Inc.	*salt and pepper shakers*
Philip Wunderle	*candies*
Harry C. Zaun	*lamps*
Zell Products Corporation	*banks*

CANADIAN DISNEY MERCHANDISE LICENSEES 1930—8

Autograph Tooth Brush Co. of Canada Ltd	*toothbrushes*
W.A. Brophey Co. Ltd	*umbrellas*
Canadian General Rubber Co. Ltd	*balloons*
Canadian Pad & Paper Co. Ltd	*pads and exercise books*
Cohn & Rosenburger Co. of Canada Ltd	*children's jewelry*
William E. Coutts Co. Ltd	*greeting cards*
Dennison Manufacturing Co. Ltd	*party novelties*
Dixon Pencil Co. Ltd	*pencils and pencil boxes*
Eastern Hat & Cap Manufacturing Co. Ltd	*children's hat and scarf sets*
General Foods Ltd	*Post Toasties*
Herbert Hosiery Mills Ltd	*children's hosiery*
International Silver Co. Ltd	*silverware*
Musson Book Co. Ltd	*books*
William Paterson Ltd	*confectionery*
Reliable Toy Co. Ltd	*stuffed dolls*
Seiberling Rubber Co. of Canada Ltd	*hot-water bottles*
A. Stein & Co. Ltd	*belts and neckwear*
Telfer Paper Box Co. Ltd	*games*
Victor Talking Machine Co. of Canada Ltd	*records*
Western Glove Works Ltd	*gloves and overalls*
George Weston Co. Ltd	*health food*
Wragge Shoe Co. Ltd	*children's footwear*

U.K. DISNEY MERCHANDISE LICENSEES 1930—8

Addis Brush Works	*toothbrushes, nailbrushes, etc.*
Amex Company	*embossed Christmas figures*
Asher, Jones and Company	*toilet articles*
Atlas Works (Wales Ltd)	*mattresses*
Bairns-Wear Yarns Ltd	*oil baize*
F. Baker & Sons	*dancing toys*
William Baker	*slumberwear*
Frederick Ball	*fancy goods*
James Barnes Ltd	*hosiery*
Barratt	*Christmas crackers, sweets*
A. & H. Bassat	*razor blades*
F. Bender & Co.	*paper doilies*
Birn Brothers Ltd	*books*
A. H. Bisby & Company	*cutlery*
Blond Brothers	*scarfs*
British Broadcasting Corporation	*music and records*
British Fondants Ltd	*confectionery*
British Thomson-Houston Co. Ltd	*Christmas tree electric lights*
British Thread Mills Ltd	*textiles*
British Xylonite Co. Ltd	*fancy goods, toilet articles*
Ralph Brown Ltd	*electro- and gold-plated non-jewelry items*
Carpet Agencies	*carpets*
Cascelloid Ltd	*celluloid novelties*
A.C. Cavalier & Co. Ltd	*toys and children's clothes*
Cave and Easterling Ltd	*rubber balls (Murray & Ramsden Ltd) and printing sets (Pneumatic Rubber Stamp Co Ltd)*
Chad Valley Co. Ltd	*toys and games*
F. Chambers & Co. Ltd	*pencils*
John B. Champion & Sons (Dursley) Ltd	*furniture*
Chappell & Co. Ltd	*music*
Charbens & Co. Ltd	*hoopla sets, games and paint sets*
David J. Clark	*stationery*
F.S. Cleaver & Sons Ltd	*fancy goods and soap*
William Collins Sons & Co. Ltd	*books and stationery*
Columbia Products	*waterproof bags*
Cooke Brothers Ltd	*brassware*
W.H. Cornelius	*printed transfers and paper goods*
R. Crook & Co.	*cycle and club pennants*
Crosse & Blackwell Ltd	*confectionery and marmalade*

Dean & Son Ltd	books
Dean's Rag Book Co. Ltd	toys, dolls and rag books
The Decca Record Co. Ltd	records
Deighton Brothers Ltd	embroidered cushions
G. Delgado Ltd	stationery
Mark Doniger (Quilts) Ltd	cot quilts and pram covers
Dudley & Co. Ltd	decorative friezes
Edmonds Brothers Ltd	novelty leather goods
Einson-Freeman	masks
Ensign Ltd	projectors and lantern slides
Field (J.C. & J. Field Ltd)	soap
S. Fielding & Co. (Devon Pottery)	chinaware
M.C. Foister, Clay & Ward Ltd	hosiery
Richard W. Foote Ltd	electric lamps and shades
Frears Ltd	biscuits
Jack Frost Ltd	Christmas crackers and toys
Fulford-Brown Brothers Ltd	silver charms
Robert Gardner & Co. Ltd	oil baize
General Foods	cereal packages
Goldhill	clockwork toys (Japanese manufacture)
The Gramophone Company Ltd	records
Grape-Nuts Co. Ltd	Post Toasties Corn Flakes
Greenwood & Cooper Ltd	children's satchels and purses
Gross & Schild	toys
H.M.V.	records
W. Hands & Sons	children's furniture
D. Harris & Co.	soap models
W.J. Harris & Co.	children's toy chairs
Higham-Tong Ltd	drapery and cotton goods
Charles Horner Ltd	jewelry
Hoyles (Ilex) Ltd	felt slippers
Holyle, Hoyle & Co. Ltd	slippers and shoes
Sydney M. Hyman	plastic models
Ideal Films Ltd	toys, novelties and books
Ingersoll Ltd	watches and clocks
Ingrams	clocks
International Art Company	postcards and calendars
International Bottle Company	perfumery bottles
Irwin Dash Music Publishing Co.	music and records
Jackson & Co.	toilet articles
Japan Traders Ltd	raffia straw bags
Walter Jelinek	novelty jewelry
Samuel Jones & Co. Ltd	stationery
Kangol Ltd	hosiery
M. Kenner	chinaware (egg cups, etc.)
Lewis Knight Ltd	balloons
Samuel Lament & Sons	sheets and pillowcases
Jules Lang & Son	children's slippers and babies' shoes
Langheck & Co. Ltd	chocolate cartons
L.A.S. Ltd	displays and cut-outs
G. Leonardi Ltd	plaster figures
Lines Brothers (Tri-ang)	children's furniture and toys
Mason & Church	Christmas crackers
S. Maw Son & Sons Ltd	miscellaneous rubber and dry goods, china figures and toothbrush holders
L.S. Mayer	toothbrush holders
Mundet Cork Products Ltd	fancy goods
Murray & Ramsden Ltd	toys
New Made Food Supplies	chocolate squares
Orel-Micro Electric	clocks
Paper Novelties Ltd	paper garlands and festoons
Paragon China Ltd	chinaware
Harold Parkinson & Associates	handkerchiefs
Pathescope Ltd	projectors and films
Paton Calvert & Co. Ltd	metal toys
George Payne & Co. Ltd	confectionery and food
Pneumatic Rubber Stamp	picture and printing sets
Price's Patent Candle Company	night lights and candles
Keith Prowse & Co. Ltd	music and records
S. D. Rand	fancy goods
L. Rees & Co. Ltd	projectors
Rubber Novelties Co. Ltd	rubber air balloons
Arthur Sanderson & Sons Ltd	wallpaper, stationery and paper products
Sol. Schaverien & Sons Ltd	umbrellas
Seftons Ltd	handkerchiefs and children's dress fabrics
Sellman & Hill Ltd	jelly moulds
George Seymour	fancy goods and cast metal car mascots
E. Sharp & Sons Ltd	confectionery
Silko Textiles	children's dress fabrics
Spear & Son	games
David Stiebel	celluloid figures and rattles
Stoddarts Ltd	lead figures
Storey Brothers & Co. Ltd	terry goods and oil baize
Swan Mill Paper Company	serviettes and tablecloths
Tabard	nursery fireplaces and portable electric heaters
E. Tanner & Co.	embroidered motifs
Tubbs, Lewis & Co.	textiles
Valentine & Sons Ltd	greeting cards
L.J. Veen's	books
Wade Heath & Co. Ltd	chinaware
Wall Paper Manufacturers Ltd	wallpapers and cretonnes
Joseph Wells & Sons Ltd	fireworks
F. Weintraub & Co.	jewelry
A. Wells & Co. Ltd	circus train and handcar toys
Whitworth & Mitchell	cotton goods
Willbank Publications Ltd	books and publications
Willsons	cut-outs and paper novelties
The Wragge Shoe Company Ltd	footwear
Wright & Son Ltd	biscuits